I0815191

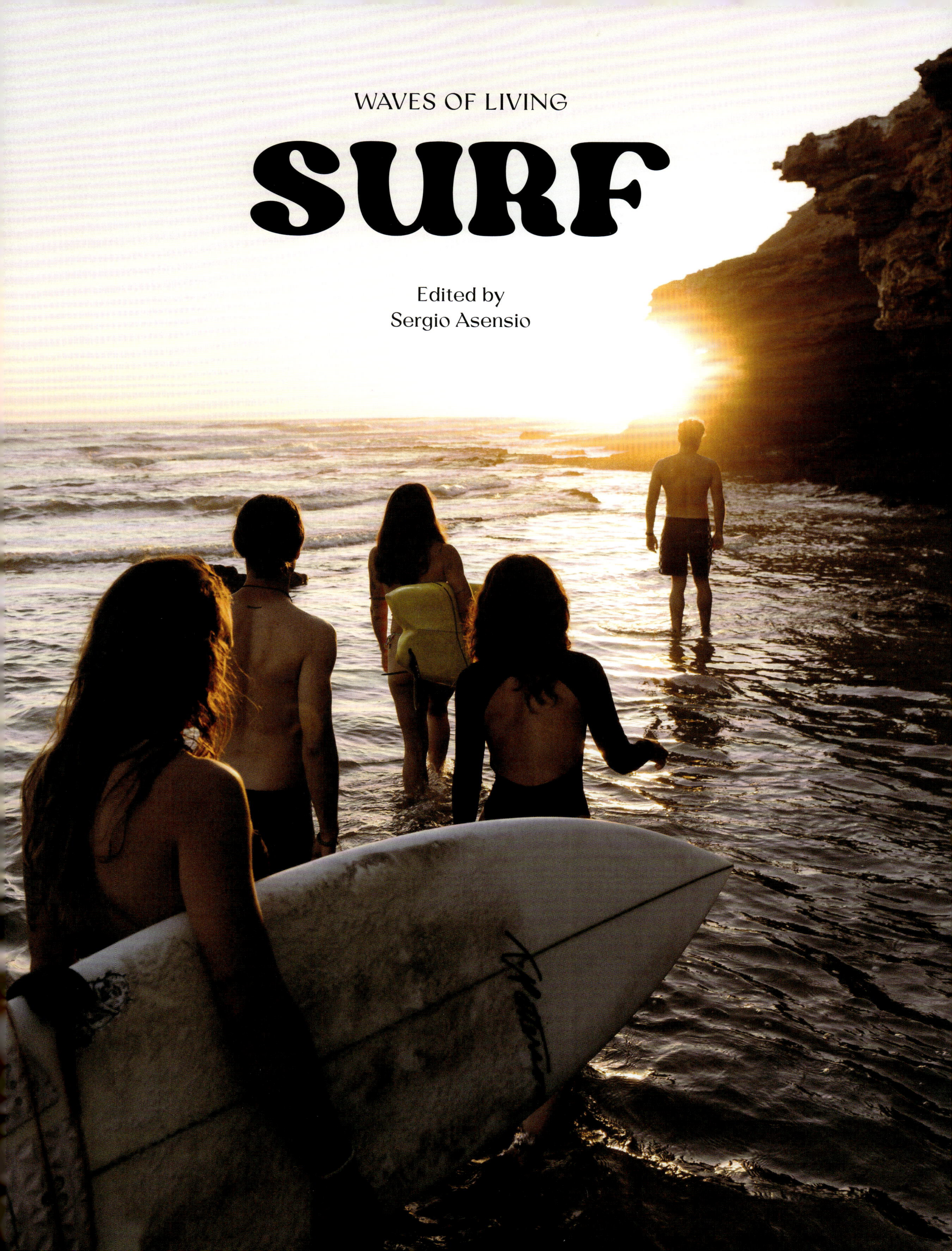

WAVES OF LIVING

SURF

Edited by
Sergio Asensio

Editorial project:
2024 © **booq** publishing, S.L.
c/ Domènech, 7-9, 2º 1ª
08012 Barcelona, Spain
T: +34 93 268 80 88
www.booqpublishing.com

ISBN: 978-84-9936-640-1

Editorial coordinator and layout:
Claudia Martínez Alonso

Editor:
Sergio Asensio

Translation:
booq publishing, S.L.

Printing in Spain

INDEX

Introduction

BEYOND THE WAVES: SURFING AS A LIFE PHILOSOPHY

Surfing is more than just a sport; it represents a comprehensive lifestyle and philosophy that integrates deeply into personal and collective identities. It goes beyond the physical act of riding waves, offering a unique perspective on life and fostering a profound connection with nature. This text delves into the significance of surfing as a passion and its role in defining individual and community identities.

Surfing embodies the essence of freedom, found in the rhythmic patterns of the sea and the dynamic interaction with waves. It is an activity that promotes respect for and understanding of the natural world, encouraging participants to harmonize with the ocean's cycles. The relationship surfers develop with the sea serves as a pathway to self-discovery and a greater appreciation of their environment.

This book presents narratives from individuals, businesses, and organizations deeply intertwined with surfing, illustrating how it functions as more than leisure. It emerges as a force for transformation, fostering community building and inspiring innovation. These narratives showcase surfing's capacity to facilitate personal growth and societal progress.

We explore how surfing impacts individuals' worldviews, influencing their decision-making, career paths, and interpersonal relationships. The principles and ethos of surfing are also seen influencing corporate and organizational cultures, promoting environments where passion and purpose converge. At its core, surfing is a pursuit of balance, offering lessons in navigating life's challenges with grace and resilience. It serves as a life metaphor, teaching adaptability, resilience, and the appreciation of tranquil moments.

This book pays homage to the surfing lifestyle, inviting readers to consider how the lessons learned on the waves permeate all facets of life, influencing thoughts, emotions, and actions. It positions surfing as not just a physical activity but a holistic approach to living. Welcome to a narrative where surfing is equated with a full, engaged life.

To Arturo, once again

As every summer, the distinctive light of Tarifa purifies the mountains, leaving the windmills behind and revealing the distant coast of Morocco on the horizon. By my side is my brother Paquito; on the other, our friend Arturo. The three of us, clad in wetsuits, prepare ourselves on the shore of El Palmar Beach, gazing at the foam breaking close by, filled with anticipation for the moment we will ride them.

Although the summer waves aren't large, we dive in with enthusiasm. Effortlessly, we reach the peak. They, more skilled, carry short and agile boards. I, on the other hand, manage the Maverick, an imposing board that Arturo's father tried to use to start surfing, without success. Its size and difficulty to transport, perhaps, gave me an advantage in catching more waves, though without performing any great feats...

After many hours at sea, with scarce waves, we are forced to exit. My father, parked in a precarious manner, waits to take us to Valdevaqueros Beach. He greets us with his typical "Cutbacks change!", a joke that only he truly understood.

At Valdevaqueros, Arturo greets his dog Lolo, resting in the shade of his father's famous trailer, decorated with surf, windsurf, and Bob Marley stickers. Beyond, on the dry grass that separates the parking from the beach, we see Arturo's father, arms akimbo and gaze on the horizon, pondering which sail to choose for windsurfing. It seems he's in dialogue with the wind, in search of the perfect sail. His welcome is warm, as if we hadn't seen each other that same morning.

Arturo, both father and son, begin to prepare their sails and boards. Meanwhile, my brother, my father, and I take turns with the rented equipment, enjoying both navigating the waves and watching each other do it. It's a unique experience.

Once at the hotel, we meet with the three families from Barcelona, with whom we share this summer tradition in Tarifa, including the Arturos. We would dine together, eagerly sharing the day's experiences. It's a moment of camaraderie, where the day's anecdotes and shared passions intertwine, fueling the desire to do it all again the next day.

These are my surfing experiences, my memories, my way of enjoying this sport. I may never have risen to professional prominence, but I have always known how to enjoy and immerse myself in its culture and dynamics. I am deeply grateful to both Arturos, father and son, for instilling in me their passion for surfing.

BLUE WAVES SURF HOUSE

THE MOROCCAN SURF VIBE

In 2014, in the heart of the vibrant Agadir region, Blue Waves Surf House was born, the fruit of the vision and passion of its founder, Tono, an aspiring agronomist who, in the course of his final year of university, discovered not only the waves but also the essence of a life shared through surfing, haunting sunsets and the warmth of local hospitality. It was in Anza, a picturesque town known for its welcoming community and captivating landscapes, where Tono found the inspiration to bring her dream to life.

With the completion of his studies and a spirit seized by the desire to share the richness of Moroccan culture, surfing and a lifestyle in harmony with nature, Tono gave birth to Blue Waves Surf House. This project, conceived with meticulous attention and a deep commitment to the well-being of the local community, sought not only to provide a haven for surf lovers but also to foster the economic and social development of Anza, using surfing as a catalyst for change and progress. More than just an accommodation, Blue Waves Surf House has become a sanctuary for surfers seeking a unique experience in Moroccan culture.

Located between the villages of Anza and Tamraght, offers a total immersion in the spirit of surfing, complemented by lessons to master the waves, yoga sessions for spiritual and emotional balance, adventures in the vastness of the desert and a unique opportunity to integrate into the daily life of the local community. The proposal Blue Waves Surf House transcends the practice of surfing; invites guests to learn about Morocco, its people and its surf.

RIPCURL

MOVJA
APPARTEMENTS
MISSA HOME

ANZA SURF HOUSE

TRADITION, CULTURE, AND SURF JUST A STEP AWAY

Located near the city of Agadir and only 13 km from the renowned surf spots of Taghazout, is Anza, a picturesque fishing village where its people and the growing surf culture create the perfect setting to know the way of living the surf of its people. Anza's surfing stands out as one of the most reliable in the region, offering ideal conditions for both learning to surf and enjoying high level waves.

Blue Waves' Anza accommodation is conveniently located about 50 meters from the most important surf spot, making it easy for guests to put on their wetsuits, grab their boards and hit the waves. This house has an incredible lounge area where guests can enjoy breathtaking sunsets over the waves while enjoying a cup of tea.

BLUE WAVES

ULTRA

"Surfing is not a sport, it's a way of life. It gives you an inexplicable connection with nature."

Gerry Lopez

TAMRAGHT SURF HOUSE

MOROCCAN OASIS FOR SURFING THRILLS AND COASTAL COMFORTS

Located in Tamraght, a charming village known for its authentic atmosphere and unparalleled hospitality, this surfer's retreat offers much more than just accommodation. Here, surf aficionados can fully immerse themselves in the surf culture, from exploring renowned surf spots to relaxing on the terrace in the sun. Here, time stands still, allowing visitors to completely unwind and live to the rhythm of the sea and the waves.

Tamraght stands proudly on a hill, offering spectacular views of the vast ocean. Located just 14 kilometers from Agadir and 3 kilometers from Taghazout, this village is not only welcoming for its people, but is also celebrated for its thriving surf culture, making it the perfect destination for surfers of all levels. With direct access to eight world-famous surf spots and close proximity to beaches such as Banana, Spider and Devil's Rock, famous for their consistent swell, Tamraght is the ideal setting for an unforgettable surfing experience. This retreat in Tamraght guarantees not only an escape from everyday life but also the opportunity to experience surfing at its purest, complemented by a climate that ensures sunny days almost all year round, adding up to 330 days of sunshine.

DOCKERS

The environment fuses surfing, yoga and relaxation, creating an ideal sanctuary for surfers of all levels, where action in the sea and tranquility on land come together perfectly.

WAVES AND CULTURE

THE ESSENCE OF SURF AND MOROCCAN TRADITION AT BLUE WAVES SURF HOUSE

At Blue Waves, the surfing experience is intimately intertwined with a deep immersion in the culture and traditions of Morocco. This approach goes beyond the teaching and practice of surfing, seeking to connect surfers with the rich diversity of Moroccan landscapes, traditions and cultures. The true essence of this experience lies not only in the connection with the sea, but also in the bond with the people and their environment.

Direct interaction with the friendly inhabitants of the nearby villages plays a fundamental role in this process of cultural immersion. Through genuine conversations, sharing traditional foods and participating in local festivities, visitors gain a deep and personal understanding of Moroccan life. These enriching experiences are complemented by visits to historic cities such as Marrakech and Essaouira, as well as explorations to picturesque Taroudant and adventures in the small desert of Massa, offering a broad perspective of Moroccan heritage. These activities are designed to complement the surfing experience, allowing visitors to explore the natural beauty of Morocco and further understand their surroundings.

This holistic approach, which combines surfing with deep cultural exploration and meaningful human connections, offers a unique window into the way Moroccans live and experience surfing. By integrating the sport with an in-depth approach to the local culture and way of life, visitors not only improve their surfing skills, but are also enriched with a deep understanding of the Moroccan passion for the sport, ensuring an enriching experience that reveals the different ways of living surfing.

34
20662

"Morocco is an open book, and its history is written in every alley, in every corner, revealing the complexity and richness of its past and present."

Fatema Mernissi

ALAÏA GROUP

REVOLUTIONIZING SURFING

In 2015, under the inspiration of the vibrant surf scene in Hossegor, France, Adam Bonvin founded the ALAÏA Group, with the vision of bringing the spirit, energy and values of surfing and action sports to Switzerland. The name "Alaïa", which pays homage to traditional Hawaiian surfboards, symbolizes the deep connection to surfing, skateboarding and snowboarding, and perfectly defines the mission to create spaces dedicated to the passion for these sports.

With the initial impetus of a crowdfunding campaign that managed to raise over 100,000 Swiss francs in less than 50 days in March 2016, ALAÏA Group came to life and began to materialize its vision. It stands out for its multifunctional complex, which includes a skatepark, big air areas, gym and trampolines, offering a comprehensive experience for extreme sports lovers.

One of its most significant achievements is Alaïa Bay, located in the Domaine des Îles recreational area, which has become the first surfing pool in Europe. This milestone not only provides a space for the surfing community, but also represents a crucial breakthrough in the accessibility and democratization of surfing on the continent, offering perfect wave conditions all year round.

In addition, the ALAÏA Group redefines the extreme sports experience by allowing enthusiasts to surf, skate and snowboard in a single day, challenging adventurers to live unique experiences in the spectacular Swiss environment. This innovative proposal reflects ALAÏA's commitment to adventure and the evolution of sport, positioning itself as an essential reference point for those seeking thrills and unprecedented experiences.

ALAÏA BAY

THE POOL OF FUTURE WAVES

In the astonishing realm of surfing, innovation reaches its zenith at Alaïa Bay, located in the heart of Switzerland. With 8,300 square meters and 13,000 cubic meters of crystal-clear water, this facility not only redefines the geography of surfing but also incorporates cutting-edge technology thanks to Wavegarden Cove, generating perfect waves that simulate the best marine conditions. This commitment to excellence extends to its ecological focus, prioritizing the use of green energy and minimizing chemical dependence, demonstrating an effort to harmonize technological innovation with environmental sustainability.

Alaïa Bay stands as a temple for surfers, offering a duality of left and right-hand waves, complemented by a specialized shop, a restaurant that captures the essence of surfing, and a school dedicated to teaching this discipline. The Shaping Room invites visitors to explore the art behind the manufacturing and repairing of boards, adding an educational layer to the experience. Alaïa Bay is not only a testament to Switzerland's passion for surfing but also a convergence of fun, sustainability, and education, all situated in a unique Alpine setting.

This Swiss gem is an invitation to live surfing comprehensively, merging the adventurous spirit with respect for the planet, promoting a culture of respect for nature, and fostering an inclusive and educational community around the sport of surfing.

A landscape that blends adrenaline and tranquility. Here, surfers catch perfect waves with majestic peaks in the background. An unparalleled experience that combines the harmony of nature with the excitement of surfing.

ALAIA
BAY
WAVE
GARDEN

“The true innovation in surfing is to modernize our sport without losing sight of our core values, opening new waves of possibilities while holding steadfast to our connection with the past.”

Adam Bonvin

Powered by WAVEGARDEN®

Powered by WAVEGARDEN

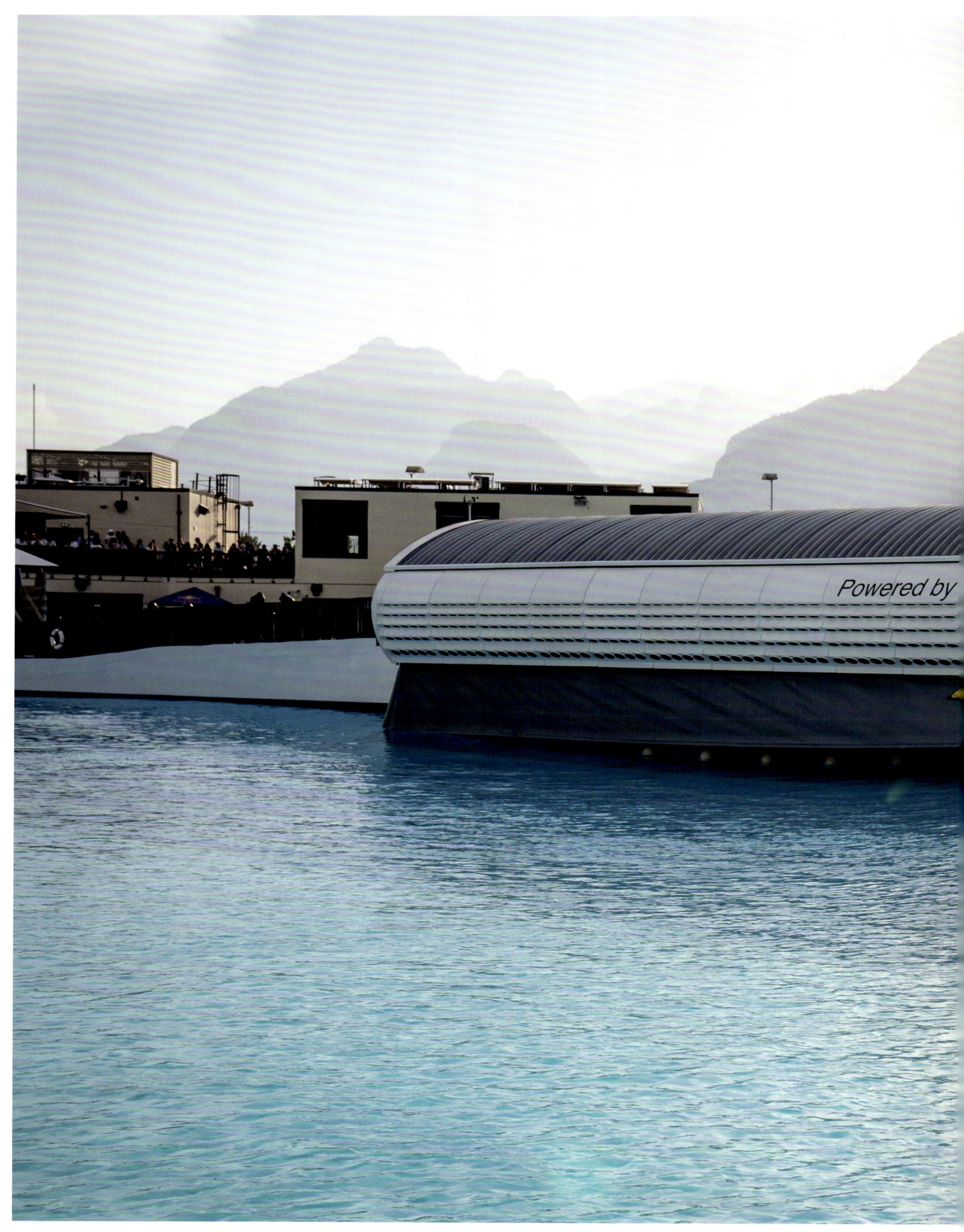
Powered by

GARDEN®

“The foam is your friend. Don't be afraid. A little extra volume here and there is good for the soul and for your surfing.”

Rob Machado

MONTANA

MONTANA

SURF, SKATE, AND SNOW ON THE SAME DAY

AN ADVENTURE FOR THE BOLDEST

ALAÏA Group has revolutionized the landscape of action sports in Switzerland, introducing a unique proposition that allows enthusiasts to experience the thrill of surfing, skateboarding, and snowboarding all in one day. This unique concept not only provides an unparalleled experience for adrenaline enthusiasts but also sets a new standard for versatility and accessibility in the world of extreme sports.

The journey begins at Alaïa Bay, where technical innovations have created optimal surfing conditions year-round. Here, both beginners and advanced surfers have the opportunity to tackle waves designed to replicate the perfection of the most coveted seas, marking the start of an unmatched day of sporting adventures.

The experience is further enriched in Crans-Montana, home to an exceptional skatepark managed by the ALAÏA Group. This space is equipped with ramps and obstacles of varying difficulty levels, designed to stimulate and challenge skaters of all ages and experience levels. The high-quality infrastructure ensures a safe and stimulating environment for skateboarding practice and improvement.

Culminating this journey, ALAÏA's snowpark, spanning over a vast area of more than 100,000 square meters, promises an unparalleled snowboarding and skiing experience. The magnitude of this space, exceptional even on a global scale, allows visitors to immerse themselves in Alpine winter, enjoying meticulously maintained slopes and terrain features designed to maximize enjoyment and safety in the snow.

In summary, ALAÏA Group has not only succeeded in integrating three of the most exciting board sports into a daily experience but has also redefined the concept of sports adventure in Switzerland. This innovative approach reflects a profound commitment to promoting sports and adventure, offering a haven for those looking to push their limits and explore new dimensions of adrenaline and sports performance.

swatch

The imposing snowpark, which covers an area of 100,000 square meters, has been carefully designed as a sanctuary for ski and snowboard enthusiasts. Its structure seeks to unleash the adrenaline of those eager for strong emotions.

ALAÏA ALPINE ALTERNATIVE

FASHIONING TOMORROW WITH SUSTAINABLE STYLE

Alaïa stands out in the world of board sports, fusing innovation, quality and sustainability. Originating in the Swiss Alps and forged by the vision of the Alaïa Group, this brand transcends the traditional concept of equipment to become a lifestyle emblem for surfers, skateboarders and snowboarders passionate about adventure and respect for the environment.

From its cradle in Sion, Switzerland, Alaïa draws inspiration from the breathtaking alpine landscape to create gear that is not only functional and durable, but also respectful of nature. It offers a range of products from innovative surfboards to clothing and accessories designed for maximum performance in extreme conditions, always with an eye toward minimizing environmental impact.

Alaïa redefines the board sports experience by integrating cutting-edge technology and performance-driven designs, ensuring that each product not only meets the expectations of the most demanding athletes but also drives the evolution of surfing and related sports. This combination of superior quality and ecological commitment positions Alaïa as a revolutionary force in the industry, inviting athletes to challenge their limits while protecting the planet.

Exclusive collaboration with European manufacturers, selected for their ecological and ethical practices, underscores Alaïa's commitment to sustainability. Every step of the process, from design to final packaging, is imbued with this philosophy, ensuring that Alaïa products are not only resilient and reliable, but also bear a legacy of environmental responsibility.

SSIMS HANDCRAFTED IN ALAIA BAY MADE

MARIONA PUJOL MERINO

SURF, CAMERA, ACTION!

Mariona, a prominent influencer in the surfing world, began forging her deep connection to the sport at the age of thirteen. Her introduction to surfing took place on the idyllic beaches of Fuerteventura, where initial contact with the sun-drenched waves catalyzed an unbreakable bond with the ocean. Raised in a family environment that celebrated freedom and adventure, Mariona has embodied these values through a life dedicated to exploration and the relentless discovery of new surfing cultures and techniques.

The global pandemic and subsequent quarantine periods offered Mariona a unique opportunity to diversify her influence, leveraging her innate storytelling talent and a magnetic presence in front of the camera. Employing digital platforms such as TikTok and Instagram, Mariona has shared snippets of adventures and surfing with the world, amassing over 1.5 million followers on TikTok and 250,000 on Instagram. Her approach, which stands out for its authenticity and limitless creativity, opens a window to a dimension where every adventure carries a story, a dream, or a life lesson.

She has surfed the waves of destinations as varied as Hawaii, Nicaragua, Panama and China, enriching her tapestry of experiences with every ridge and valley traversed. Mariona's story is a vibrant testament to how surfing, in its purest essence, is a vehicle for adventure, self-knowledge and human connection, inviting all those touched by its magic to pursue their passions beyond any known horizon.

THE JOURNEY OF A SURFING INFLUENCER

INTERVIEW WITH MARIONA PUJOL

Can you recall your first time surfing? How was that experience, and what drove you to continue exploring the world of surfing?

The first time I ventured into the world of surfing was in Fuerteventura, during a family trip at the age of 13. We rented boards and had the guidance of an instructor who taught us the essentials. Although I immensely enjoyed the experience, it was somewhat challenging, as the waves proved to be imposing and difficult to catch for a beginner like me. Despite the initial frustration, that day marked the beginning of my fascination with surfing.

There was a moment when you took the step to start recording and sharing content. How did that decision come about, and how has it changed your life since then?

The moment I decided to start recording myself and sharing content was more of a natural progression than a specific step. I can't recall the exact first moment, as I used to record myself talking in front of the camera since my childhood. However, during the quarantine, I decided to take it a step further and begin sharing those videos on my social media. That's when I quickly discovered that people enjoyed my content. It was quite straightforward.

Your social media content is known for being quick and entertaining. What do you believe is the secret to capturing your followers' attention? Is there an anecdote behind a post that was particularly fun to create?

I believe the key lies in doing something different. In a world saturated with repetitive content, I chose to showcase my personality from the start. I think the key is to be authentic and true to oneself. Only then will followers enjoy the content as much as I enjoy creating it.

With 1.5 million on TikTok and 220,000 on Instagram (and counting), how do you handle having so many followers on social media? Has it been overwhelming at times, or have you always enjoyed the journey?

Yes, they are many followers! At times, I'm not fully aware of the responsibility it carries. I try to keep things in perspective, thinking that I have the opportunity to positively influence my followers. My goal is to motivate people to exercise and enjoy real life.

Beyond being an activity, surfing seems to be a fundamental part of your life. How would you define what surfing means to you and how has it influenced the person you've become?

Surfing isn't just a sport for me; it's a complete escape. The anticipation of catching waves intensifies due to the sporadic opportunities. It has woven a thread of positivity throughout my life, fostering lasting friendships, thrilling travel adventures, and unforgettable experiences. I can't recall visiting a place where surfing wasn't possible; it's become an integral part of my journeys. Surfing isn't just a pastime; it's a lifestyle.

Besides extreme sports, is there another passion or interest that deeply excites you? Something that might surprise your followers to know about you?

Absolutely! While extreme sports are my public passion, there's another side of my life that doesn't often make it onto social media. I absolutely love spending time with my family; they are a fundamental pillar in my life. On top of that, there's a culinary side to me that many might not know about—I thoroughly enjoy cooking. And yes, I'm also immersed in my university studies. While it might not be a burning passion, not everything in life can be about travel and extreme sports.

You've traveled to many places. What has been your favorite destination for surfing so far? Is there a place still on your wish list?

At 21, I've had the fortune to explore various destinations, although perhaps fewer than I would like. Among my top 3 for surfing are Hawaii, Nicaragua, and Panama. However, my wish list continues to grow, with places like the Philippines, Australia, the Maldives, and Bali on the horizon. Curiosity leads me to consider moving to Australia once I finish my degree. Additionally, I have a particular desire to surf in Japan, a destination I believe is underrated in the world of surfing.

Can you share a particular experience that has been unforgettable for you? Whether due to excitement, the beauty of the place, or any other reason that left a mark.
Definitely, being in China with my skate team was an incredible experience. The immersion in the culture, the connection with the people, and the delicious gastronomy were aspects that left an indelible mark. I even had amusing moments being stopped for photos just because I was a foreigner. Although I tried surfing, the waves weren't at their best, but the overall experience was simply great.

Along your journey so far, what stands out for you? What has left the most significant mark on your personal and professional journey?
Definitely, I cherish the people I've had the fortune to meet thanks to surfing. I don't know where I would be today without my friends. I've always said it, and I stand by it: human connections are the most valuable treasure I've found on my journey, both personally and professionally.

Looking ahead, are there any exciting projects or goals you've set that you can share? What can we expect from Mariona Pujol in the coming months or years?
Always thinking ahead, I have numerous projects and motivations to continue growing and reinventing myself. I'd rather not spill the beans just yet to avoid jinxing them, haha! However, it's true that, while I may not see myself doing extreme sports at 50, I maintain a strong motivation to keep evolving and exploring new horizons in the coming months and years. The adventure never stops!

Mariona's life is a narrative of continuous growth, exploration, and the quest for personal evolution.

Mariona Pujol's surf odyssey spans Hawaii's legendary waves, Nicaragua's serene shores, Panama's challenging swells, and China's surprising Hainan Island, each enriching her journey with unique cultures and experiences.

"Ride the waves of life with the same passion and courage as you do in the ocean; each crest a challenge, each trough a lesson, and every horizon, a new beginning."

Mariona Pujol

ULUWATU SURF VILLAS

THE SURFING PARADISE

Located on the cliffs of southern Bali, the Uluwatu Surf Villas emerged in the surfing world in 1971, the year that saw the birth of the iconic surf movie "Morning of the Earth". This film not only captured the essence of surfing, but also inspired legends like Wayne Lynch to explore the shores of Uluwatu in search of those perfect waves. Since its inception as Bali Villas in 2001, Uluwatu Surf Villas has undergone a profound transformation, establishing itself as the destination of choice for those passionate about surfing who want to immerse themselves in an unforgettable experience in Bali.

Over time, Uluwatu Surf Villas has been able to adapt to the needs and desires of its visitors, becoming a refuge that combines the essence of surfing with a touch of "barefoot luxury". Beyond offering a place to stay, these villas invite you to live an authentic Balinese experience, enriched with sunrise yoga sessions, local adventures and even a skatepark surrounded by the lush jungle. This sanctuary, far from the hustle and bustle of everyday life, becomes a window into the exploration and enjoyment of the majestic ocean and its vibrant surroundings.

What truly distinguishes the Uluwatu Surf Villas is its exclusive access to one of the most iconic surf spots in the world, a surfer's paradise. The waves, capable of reaching impressive heights of up to 7 meters, offer the perfect setting to challenge the limits and immerse yourself in the true essence of surfing. This place not only captures the beauty and power of the ocean, but has also become the sanctuary of top surfers such as Kelly Slater, Rob Machado, or Gerry Lopez, among many others. These legendary surfing figures have left their mark on the waters of Uluwatu, raising the standard of what it means to master these monumental waves. It is not uncommon to see these icons sharing their passion and knowledge with the next generation of surfers, making Uluwatu Surf Villas a place that perfectly represents the Balinese way of surfing.

Nestled atop Bali's dramatic cliffs, Uluwatu Surf Villas boasts a prime location, offering breathtaking views of world-class surf breaks.

"Where every sunrise is a wave of opportunities, and every sunset is a journey to serenity in the surfer's paradise."

THE SPIRIT OF BALI

FROM YOGA RETREATS AND SKATE PARKS TO SUNSET WEDDINGS AND BEACHFRONT PARTIES

Uluwatu Surf Villas presents itself as an authentic reflection of the island spirit, where surf culture, the art of skateboarding and the ancient practice of yoga converge in one place. This resort, rooted in Bali's rich heritage, offers guests a deep immersion in activities that are essential to the Balinese experience, amalgamating sport, spirituality and nature.

Surfing capitalizes on the island's legendary wave reputation, providing surfers the opportunity to take on the crystal clear waters of the Indian Ocean. This sport, intrinsically linked to the Balinese lifestyle, is celebrated here not only as a recreational activity, but as a form of deep connection with the sea.

Skateboarding, on the other hand, is presented not only as an extension of surfing on land, but also as a means of exploring creativity and balance. The skate park at Uluwatu Surf Villas, designed to satisfy both beginners and experts, reflects Bali's architecture and natural landscape, creating a space where tradition and modernity meet.

Yoga is an invitation to introspection and balance, inspired by the spiritual practices that have flourished in Bali for centuries. Yoga retreats are held in serene surroundings that foster inner peace and harmony with the environment, allowing guests to reconnect with themselves and the nature that surrounds them.

Beyond these activities, Uluwatu Surf Villas offers experiences that capture the essence of Bali. From wedding ceremonies overlooking the breathtaking cliffs to vibrant beach parties celebrating local culture and music, the resort is dedicated to providing unforgettable moments that reflect the unique character of the island.

YOGA CLASSES

Uluwatu Surf Villas offers daily yoga classes designed to harmonize the body and mind. In this tranquil setting high on the cliffs, guests engage in deep yoga practice guided by experienced instructors, against a backdrop of stunning natural beauty, enhancing both well-being and surfing skills.

LEGENDS CHOICE

These villas are famous for hosting surfing icons like Kelly Slater, Rob Machado, and Gerry Lopez. This renowned destination in Bali attracts the crème de la crème of the surfing community, highlighting its status as a premier surf retreat.

DRIFTER SURF

THE BRAND OF BALINESE SURF

Bali was initially a destination for brave explorers eager to venture into its uncharted turquoise waters. Each surf session turned into an exhilarating odyssey. The island, particularly Uluwatu, rose to prominence as a haven for seasoned surfers following the release of "Morning of the Earth", a 1971 film by renowned director Alby Falzon. With the arrival of legendary Hawaiian surfer Gerry López, followed by many others, the place transformed into an epicenter for those seeking to challenge Uluwatu's impeccable barrels, reinforcing its legend.

Fast forward several decades, two surfers, after their own experiences in Bali, were inspired to establish a space that truly reflected the exciting world of surfing and its distinctive culture. Thus, in 2008, Drifter Surf was born. Initially conceived as an independent store and café, it offered essentials for surfing and outdoor activities, as well as products adorned with artwork by artists like Chris Del Moro and Andy Davis. Drifter Surf quickly became a meeting point for enthusiasts, boasting a remarkable collection of boards from legends like Terry Fitzgerald, Gerry Lopez, and Dick Brewer, resembling a living museum of surf exploration. Its offerings were complemented by a selection of books, ideal for those looking to escape the digital world, positioning Drifter as the preferred spot for sharing stories over coffee and waves.

The sustained growth of Drifter reflects the fervor of ocean lovers for activities both on the surface and in the marine depths, encompassing everything from surfing to spearfishing and environmental conservation. Today, this family-run surf brand has expanded with vibrant locations in Seminyak and Uluwatu, extending its influence beyond Bali and spreading its love for the sea.

SLIDE
OPEN

MATUSE

THE ART OF SURFING
DRIFTER
SURF
PYZEL
PYZEL
PYZEL
PYZEL
PYZEL
PYZEL

"With its golden beaches, lush rice terraces, and a rich cultural heritage, Bali offers a unique experience that blends natural beauty with spirituality rooted in every temple and friendly smile."

DRIFTER
DRIFTER

Drifter
SURF

POLEN SURFBOARDS

POLEN SURFBOARDS

INNOVATION AND TRADITION IN SURFBOARD MANUFACTURING

Polen Surfboards, founded in 1988 on the coast of Portugal, is more than just a surfboard brand; it is an entity that embodies a deep commitment to quality and innovation in the world of surfing. Since its inception, Polen has honored traditional craftsmanship in creating surfboards while simultaneously incorporating advanced technologies to enhance the surfing experience for enthusiasts of all levels, from eager beginners to seasoned professionals, always aiming to exceed their expectations.

For over three decades, Polen has strengthened its position in both the European and international surf scenes, renowned for crafting surfboards that combine functionality with unparalleled aesthetics. These boards, acclaimed in the challenging surf environments of Portugal, Australia, Hawaii, and the United States, are appreciated for their durability, high performance, and innovative design, setting new standards in the industry.

Beyond its excellence in production, Polen Surfboards actively cultivates a global community of surf enthusiasts, committed to providing boards that not only enhance skills in the water but also capture the individual essence of each surfer. This commitment to customization reflects Polen's belief that a surfboard transcends its functional purpose to become a true extension of the surfer, an ally in their journey towards mastery and personal expression in surfing. Through this approach, Polen not only supplies high-quality equipment but also fosters a sense of belonging and progress within the vast surfing community.

POLEN SURFBOARDS
SINCE 1988

THE ART OF CRAFTING SURFBOARDS

WHERE EVERY BOARD IS A MASTERPIECE OF THE ART OF SURFING

At Polen Surfboards, the production of each surfboard is approached with a meticulous focus that combines technical precision and detailed customization, emphasizing the importance of the "shaper's" art in the creation process. This process begins with the careful selection of high-quality materials, ensuring that each board is not only durable and resilient but also optimally responsive to the variable sea conditions.

Polen's "shapers," masters in the art of shaping surfboards, apply advanced techniques and deep knowledge of wave behavior to design boards that cater to the specific needs of each surfer. This design and manufacturing process involves several critical stages, from the initial sketch to the final shaping, where every detail matters to achieve the perfect balance between buoyancy, stability, and maneuverability.

Customization is a fundamental pillar in Polen Surfboards' philosophy. Recognizing that each surfer has their unique style and preferences, the shapers work closely with customers to incorporate their wishes and requirements into the final board design. This collaboration ensures that each board not only reflects the surfer's identity but also enhances their performance in the water, facilitating a deeper and more harmonious connection with the waves.

In addition to customization, Polen Surfboards is dedicated to continuous innovation in manufacturing techniques. By experimenting with new materials and technologies, such as eco-friendly resins and cutting-edge cores, Polen is constantly seeking ways to improve the sustainability and environmental impact of its products without compromising quality or performance.

POLEN SURFBOARDS
MANUFACTURING CO.

"Surfing, among other sports, elicits laughter by its very essence, as it transforms an inexplicable and useless impulse into an art and a way of life, rather than turning a skill into a competition."

Matt Warshaw

FBOARDS
OLEN
PT
INCE 1988

THE JOURNEY OF POLEN SURFBOARDS

30 YEARS OF COMMITMENT TO INNOVATION AND PASSION FOR INTERNATIONALLY ACCLAIMED SURFBOARDS

Founded in 1988, Polen Surfboards began its journey into the competitive world of surfing in Portugal, a country known for its exceptional coastline, ideal beaches and perfect waves. This strategic location not only gave Polen access to some of the best waves in Europe, but also placed the brand in the heart of a rich surf culture, from where it began to build its reputation.

From its inception, Polen set an ambitious goal: to produce the best surfboards in Europe, employing materials and techniques comparable to those of leading global surf destinations such as Australia, Hawaii and the United States. This vision helped Polen quickly differentiate itself and establish itself as a renowned brand on the European and world surfing scene.

Over the years, Polen Surfboards has witnessed remarkable growth and recognition, excelling in international competitions and winning prestigious titles that have reaffirmed its position among the surfing elite. This track record of success has not only contributed to Polen's status as a leading brand, but has also reinforced its commitment to excellence, innovation and continuous product improvement.

For more than three decades, Polen's mission has remained unchanged: to advance the progression of surfing by constantly innovating and perfecting its boards. This dedication is reflected in every aspect of their manufacturing process, from the initial design to the final product, ensuring that each board is of the highest quality and perfectly tailored to each surfer's needs and preferences. Polen understands that, for both seasoned professionals and those facing their first wave, the surfboard is not just a piece of equipment, but an extension of their experience in the water.

POLEN

POLEN

POLEN
SURF DESIGN

SURF DESIGN
POLEN

GETTING TO KNOW THE SHAPERS

THE CRAFTSMEN BEHIND POLEN SURFBOARDS

In the realm of surfing, the term "shaper" refers to highly skilled specialists responsible for designing and crafting surfboards. These professionals act as true architects of the surfing world, combining artistic skills with deep technical knowledge to create boards that perfectly suit the needs and styles of each surfer. At Polen Surfboards, shapers play a crucial role, constituting the core of the brand's identity and success. Their work goes far beyond simple board production; they are dedicated to creating custom works that reflect the preferences and personality of individual surfers.

What truly sets Polen Surfboards apart in the industry is the extraordinary dedication of its shapers. These craftsmen pay meticulous attention to every detail, from material selection to the final finish, infusing their passion into every aspect of design and manufacturing. This passion ensures that each board not only meets functional expectations but also becomes an expression of the surfer's unique identity.

Polen's shapers are known for being not only experienced artisans but also true innovators and surf enthusiasts. They possess a holistic understanding of the sport, allowing them to anticipate and respond to emerging trends, as well as adapt their designs to changing sea conditions and surfer preferences. This synergy of skill, innovation, and a passion for surfing translates into every board they produce, ensuring that each Polen Surfboards product is not only of the highest quality but also unique.

Furthermore, Polen Surfboards distinguishes itself by fostering a culture of close collaboration between shapers and surfers. This collaborative approach enables shapers to deeply understand the needs and desires of surfers, resulting in boards that are truly extensions of the individuals who use them. Thus, Polen is not merely a surfboard brand; it is a vibrant community, united by a common love for surfing and a respect for exquisite craftsmanship.

PAULO DO BAIRRO

Paulo do Bairro is a prominent figure in the first generation of professional surfers in Portugal in the early 1990s. He began his career using Polen surfboards, which played a crucial role in the successful start of his surfing journey. After years of sponsorship and working in the industry, Paulo transitioned to crafting surfboards, bringing his expertise to Polen Surfboards.

SURFBOARDS
CO

JON PYZEL

Jon Pyzel's passion for surfing led him to Oahu's North Shore, where he started his career in surfboard shaping. He learned the craft from master shaper Jeff Bushman and, over time, built a strong partnership with surfer John John Florence. Pyzel Surfboards became renowned not only for their performance but also for the loyalty and dedication of riders like John John Florence.

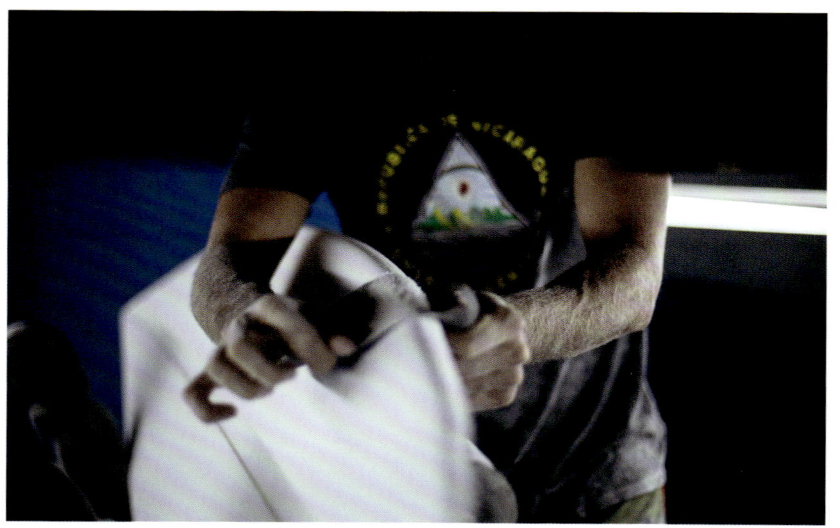

PYZEL
SPY
STANCE

BRETT WARNER

Brett Warner's surfing journey began at a young age, eventually leading him to the professional circuit and later the ASP tour. After his major sponsor folded, he decided to transition into shaping surfboards. Warner Surfboards emerged in 1996, benefiting from Brett's experience in shaping and learning from industry greats like Greg Clough.

TIMMY PATTERSON

Tim Patterson honed his shaping skills at Hobie Surfboards and worked alongside legends of the sport. Tim's experience spans all aspects of surfboard manufacturing, from design to handcrafting. His dedication to innovation and collaboration with top surfers have made T. Patterson Surfboards a highly sought-after brand worldwide.

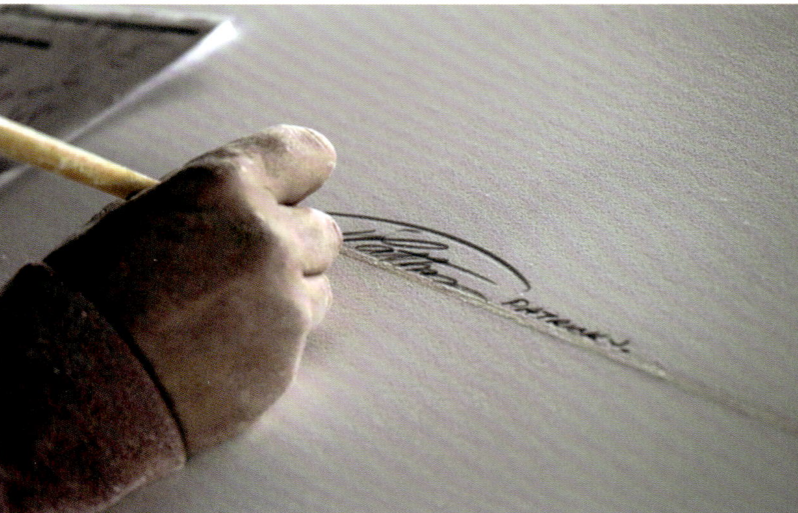

UNITED BY THE WAVES

THE TEAM

This team stands as the embodiment of the brand, serving as dedicated ambassadors who showcase the company values both in competitive arenas and in their daily pursuits. These athletes , proudly representing PolenSurfboards, form the bedrock of the brand, breathing vitality into it through their commitment, expertise, and the exceptional performance of their equipment. Together, they navigate not only the vast oceans but also the very spirit and essence of PolenSurfboards.

João Guedes

Aka: Guedes
Born: Porto
Local Spot: Porto/Ericeira
Height x Weight: 1.74 m / 76 kg
Stance: Goofy
Favorite Waves: Mentawai, Cabo Verde, Ericeira, Porto, Nazare, Galiza
Favorite Maneuvers: Barrel
Magic Boards: 6'2 POLEN Margarita
Sponsors: Deeply, POLEN, Futures
I surf because: surf is my lifestyle since I was born

Pedro Boonman

Aka: Boonman
Date of birth: 08/08/1992
Local Spot: Carcavelos
Height x Weight: 1.80 m / 73 kg
Stance: Goffy
Sponsors: Sooruz, Vonzipper, Polen Sufboards, O&E, Future Fins
Magic Boards: 5.11 Quad, Roud Pin Modelo: Margarita Polen Surfboards
Favourite wave in Portugal: Supertubos/ Nazaré

SURF COMPANIONS

BOOKS, COURSES, AND RETREATS FOR SURFERS

Born from the cresting waves of El Palmar, Surf Companions emerged as a beacon for the surf-curious and the wave-obsessed alike. It began with two distinct tales of surf passion converging in 2019—a transformative collaboration between Daniel, an avid surfer and coach with a journey rooted in New Zealand's rugged waters, and Florian, a designer whose first surf in Andalucía's gentle swells sparked a creative revolution in surf learning.

Surf Companions is the embodiment of their shared vision: to enhance the surf experience through meticulously crafted guides and educational materials. With the Intermediate Surf Companion, the pair bridged the gap between the ocean's challenges and a surfer's potential, offering illustrated wisdom that resonates with both landlocked enthusiasts and coastal experts.

Beyond the pages, the company expanded into digital realms, offering a suite of services from video tutorials to personalized coaching, all while fostering a community through surf retreats and interactive platforms. As stewards of surf culture, they continue to innovate, with plans for comprehensive guides on longboarding and advanced techniques, ensuring that the Surf Companions name remains synonymous with progression, community, and the enduring spirit of surfing.

FOUNDED IN EL PALMAR

TWO SURFING JOURNEYS CONVERGE

In the sunlit glow of Andalucia's El Palmar, the vision for Surf Companions took shape, a testament to the serendipitous fusion of two distinct surfing odysseys. It was 2019 when Daniel and Florian, from disparate surfing backgrounds, sat on a terrace with a vista of rolling waves, drafting the blueprint of an illustrated surf workbook. Daniel's journey into the surf began in the rugged waters of New Zealand in 2010, where towering waves introduced him to the sport's raw beauty and challenge. This brush with nature's untamed force only fueled his passion, steering his academic focus towards sports therapy, and eventually to becoming a seasoned surf coach.

Florian's tale was different. His first encounter with surfing occurred in 2013, in Andalucia itself, while visiting a friend. Initially indifferent to water sports, he found himself captivated after just a few lessons at a local surf school. The experience was transformative, sparking a newfound dedication to the sport.

Their paths intersected in France in 2013, but it was not until five years later that their collaboration would ignite. Florian's innovative approach to documenting his surf journey through "surf notes" caught Daniel's eye. Recognizing the potential in Florian's detailed sketches, the duo envisioned a book to guide surf enthusiasts. Thus, beneath the Andalusian sun where Florian had sketched waves and Daniel had embraced them, Surf Companions was born – a fusion of art, expertise, and a shared passion for the surf.

A serene oasis in Andalusia, El Palmar captivates with its unspoiled beauty and tranquil ambiance. This hidden gem, surrounded by lush landscapes, offers a perfect escape into nature's embrace. A visit here promises rejuvenation and an unforgettable experience in Spain's heart.

CATCHING WAVES ON PAPER

THE EVOLUTION OF A SURFER'S GUIDE

As the Andalusian waves whispered tales of adventure, Daniel and Florian laid the groundwork for what would become a seminal guide for wave riders. The chapter of creation began right after their transformative 2019 surf trip in El Palmar, with a mission to craft a manual for the intermediate surfer. Identifying a gap in the market, they targeted surfers and coaches who as- pired to elevate their craft beyond the basics. The synergistic blend of Dan- iel's deep coaching experience and Florian's artistic prowess translated into a comprehensive guide.

Armed with pencil and ink pen, Florian brought to life the intricate techniques and philosophies of surfing through his illustrations, while Daniel infused the text with insights garnered from years of teaching and riding the waves. Early prototypes of The Intermediate Surf Companion emerged from this collaborative spirit, each iteration refined through the critical eyes of the surfing community.

By October 2019, the first edition graced a local surf shop's shelves in El Palmar, marking a milestone for the duo. Opting for a climate-neutral local printer, they ensured that their ethos of sustainability echoed through their work. The initial DIY aesthetic of the book, with its spiral binding, evolved into a more polished thread binding in subsequent editions, paralleling the founders' growth and expanding vision. The Surf Companion Books were not just manuals but a catalyst for the community, continually improving with feedback and shared experiences of surf enthusiasts worldwide.

THE
BEGINNERS
SURF
COMPANION
DANIEL SPES & FLORIAN HATTICH
THE
INTERMEDIATE
SURF
COMPANION
3rd EDITION
ILLUSTRATIONS
FLORIAN HATTICH
WRITTEN BY
DANIEL SPES & FLORIAN HATTICH
EXPERTISE
DANIEL SPES

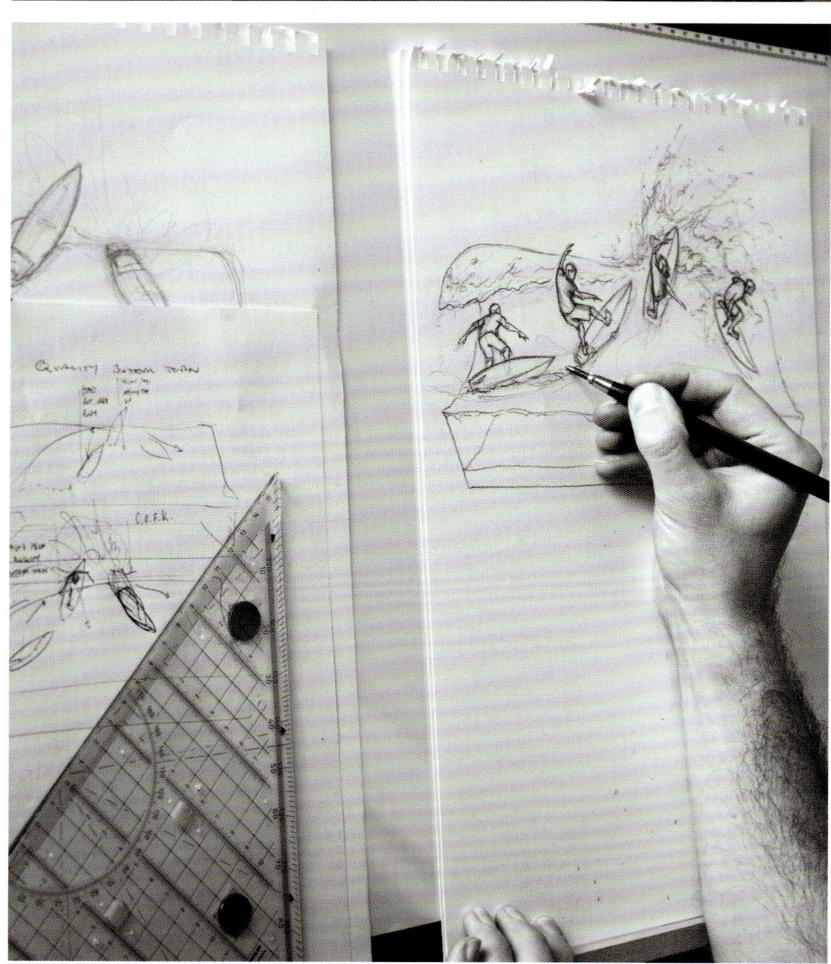

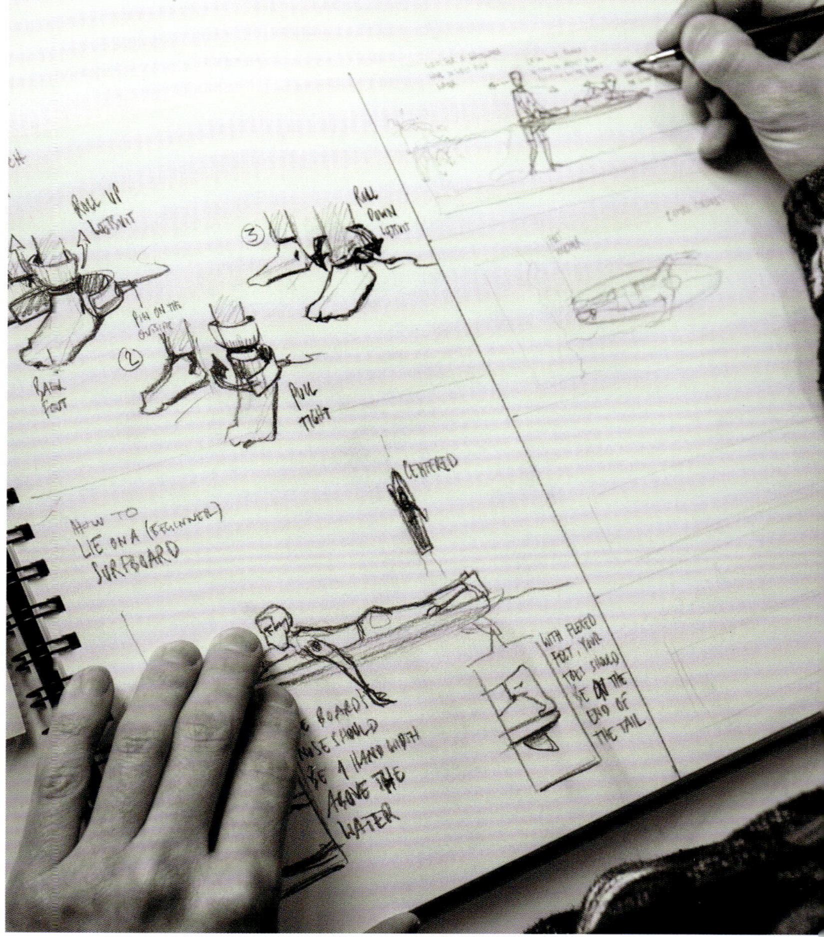

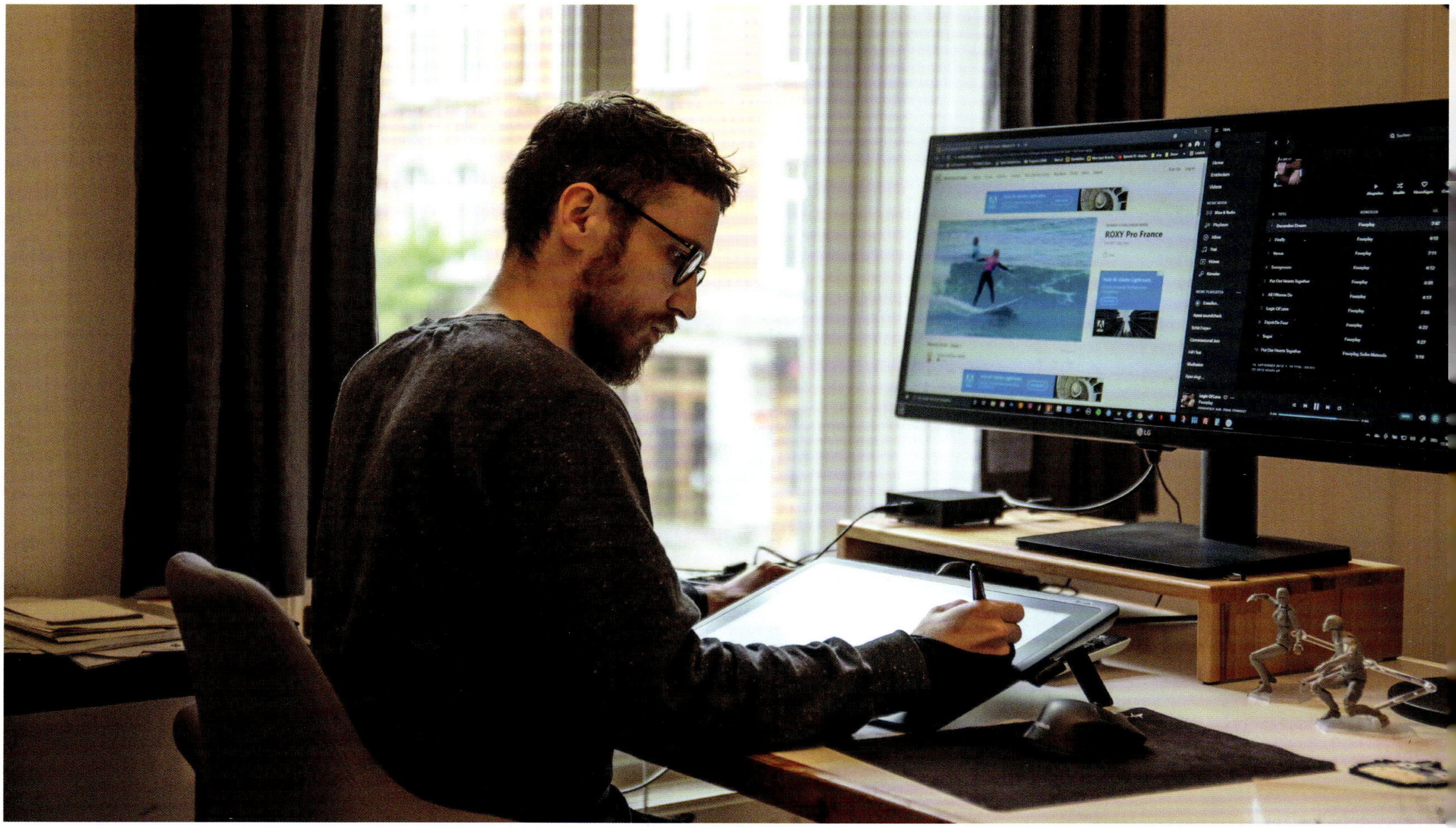
ROXY Pro France

ROLL UP LEFT FOOT
PULL DOWN LEFT FOOT
FIN ON THE OUTSIDE
RIGHT FOOT
PULL TIGHT
CENTERED
HOW TO LIE ON A (BEGINNER) SURFBOARD
WITH FLEXED FEET, YOUR TOES SHOULD BE ON THE END OF THE TAIL
BE A HAND WIDTH ABOVE THE WATER

“Surfing transcends mere sport; t's a symphony of waves and spirit, a dance with nature. It teaches humility, patience, and respect, turning the ocean's rhythm into a guide for life. Every wave, a story; every ride, a lesson.”

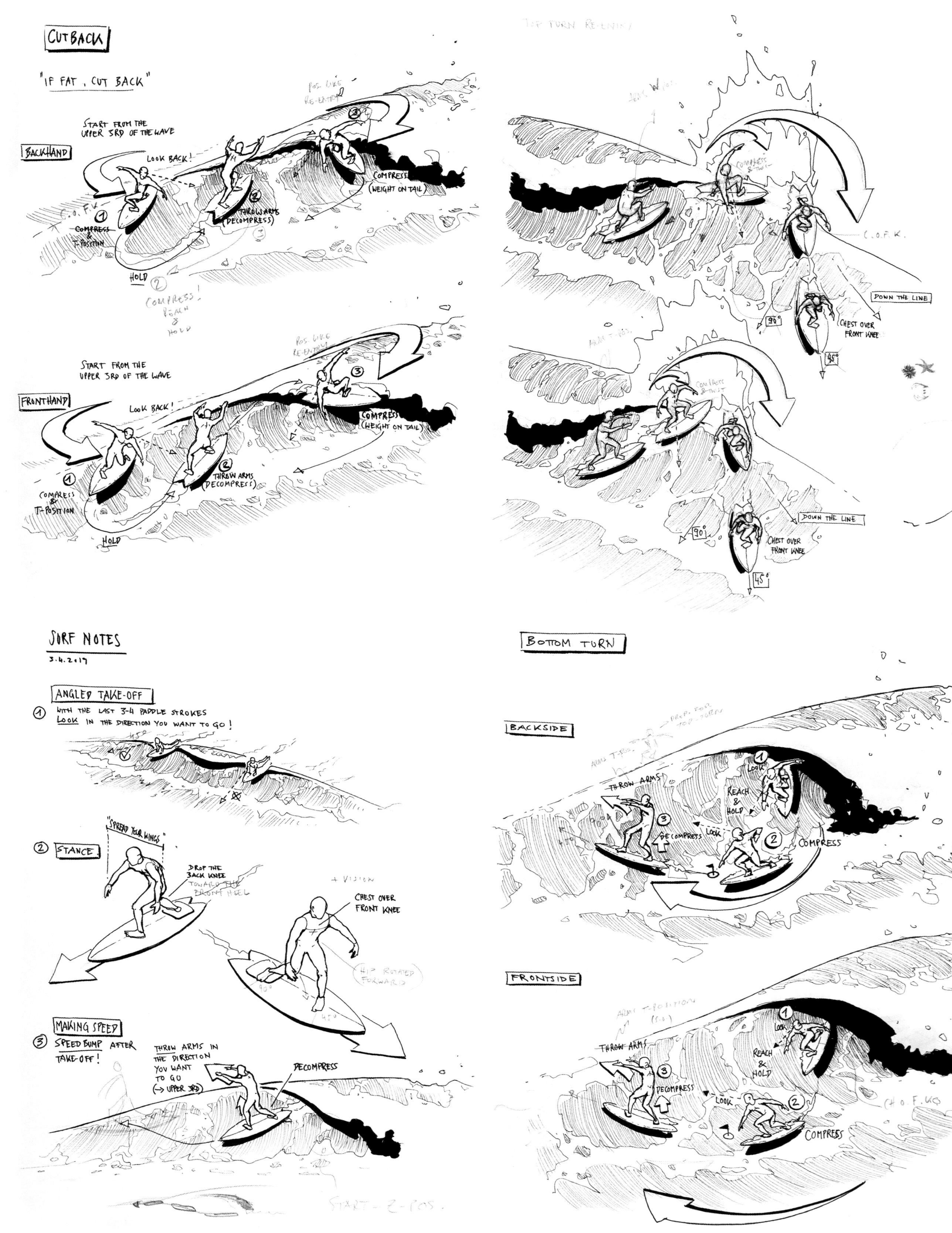

CUTBACK
"IF FAT, CUT BACK"
START FROM THE UPPER 3RD OF THE WAVE
BACKHAND
LOOK BACK!
COMPRESS & T-POSITION
THROW ARMS (DECOMPRESS)
COMPRESS (WEIGHT ON TAIL)
HOLD
START FROM THE UPPER 3RD OF THE WAVE
FRONTHAND
LOOK BACK!
COMPRESS & T-POSITION
THROW ARMS (DECOMPRESS)
COMPRESS (WEIGHT ON TAIL)
HOLD
C.O.F.K.
DOWN THE LINE
90°
CHEST OVER FRONT KNEE
45°
DOWN THE LINE
90°
CHEST OVER FRONT KNEE
45°
SURF NOTES
3.4.2017
ANGLED TAKE-OFF
1 WITH THE LAST 3-4 PADDLE STROKES LOOK IN THE DIRECTION YOU WANT TO GO!
2 STANCE
"SPREAD YOUR WINGS"
DROP THE BACK KNEE
+ VISION
CHEST OVER FRONT KNEE
MAKING SPEED
3 SPEED BUMP AFTER TAKE-OFF!
THROW ARMS IN THE DIRECTION YOU WANT TO GO (→ UPPER 3RD)
DECOMPRESS
BOTTOM TURN
BACKSIDE
THROW ARMS
1 LOOK
REACH & HOLD
3 DECOMPRESS
LOOK
2 COMPRESS
FRONTSIDE
THROW ARMS
1 LOOK
REACH & HOLD
3 DECOMPRESS
LOOK
2 COMPRESS

WETSUITS

THERE ARE MANY TYPES OF WETSUITS WITH **DIFFERENT THICKNESSES FOR DIFFERENT WATER TEMPERATURES**. IT'S GOOD TO HAVE A SUIT WITHOUT VELCRO, WHICH CAN DAMAGE THE MATERIAL IF IT GETS STUCK ON THE SUIT. WHEN BUYING A WETSUIT, BE AWARE THAT **EVERY BRAND HAS A DIFFERENT FIT**, SO SIZES MAY VARY SIGNIFICANTLY FROM ONE BRAND TO ANOTHER. IN TERMS OF MATERIAL THERE ARE MANY OPTIONS NOWADAYS, FROM CLASSIC NEOPRENE TO A WIDE SELECTION OF **ECO-FRIENDLY** ALTERNATIVES (WHICH WE DEFINITELY PREFER). THE ZIPS, TOO, COME IN MANY VARIANTS – FRONT, BACK, OR CHEST ZIP, AND EVEN COMPLETELY ZIPLESS. WITH A WETSUIT YOU REALLY GET WHAT YOU PAY FOR SO BUY THE BEST SUIT YOU CAN AFFORD AND YOU WON'T REGRET IT IN TERMS OF WARMTH, COMFORT AND DURABILITY.

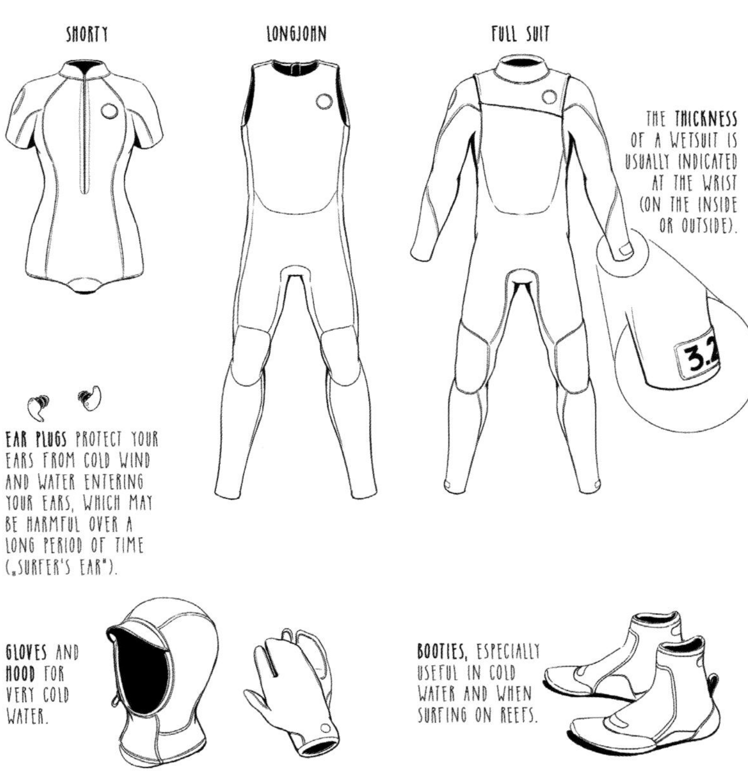

DANGER FROM HUMANS & BOARDS

THE MOST COMMON DANGERS ARE **OTHER SURFERS AND THEIR BOARDS**, AS WELL AS YOUR **OWN BOARD** AND LEASH. ONE THING YOU CAN DO TO MITIGATE THE DANGER POSED BY OTHERS IS CHOOSING A SPOT WHERE THERE ARE NOT TOO MANY OTHER SURFERS. THAT IS NOT ALWAYS AN OPTION, HOWEVER. LUCKILY, THERE ARE SOME THINGS YOU CAN DO TO AVOID ACCIDENTS WITH PEOPLE AND EQUIPMENT, BE IT THEIRS OR YOUR OWN. SO **MAKE SURE YOU KNOW WHAT TO DO** SHOULD A POTENTIALLY DANGEROUS SITUATION OCCUR.

DANGER: OTHER SURFERS

WHENEVER A SURFER LOOKS LIKE THEY'RE LOSING CONTROL OVER THEIR BOARD, MAKE SURE YOU GET OUT OF THE WAY IN TIME, IF NECESSARY BY **DIVING. PROTECT YOUR HEAD AND NECK**, AND **CURL INTO A LITTLE BALL**, SO EVEN IF YOU DO GET HIT, YOU WILL NOT GET SERIOUSLY HARMED.

DANGER: YOUR BOARD

WHEN YOU DO A NOSE DIVE, YOUR BOARD GETS PROPELLED INTO THE AIR DUE TO ITS BUOYANCY...

...WHEN IT COMES DOWN AGAIN IT MAY HIT YOUR HEAD JUST AS YOU RESURFACE. SO ALWAYS PROTECT YOUR HEAD WHEN SURFACING.

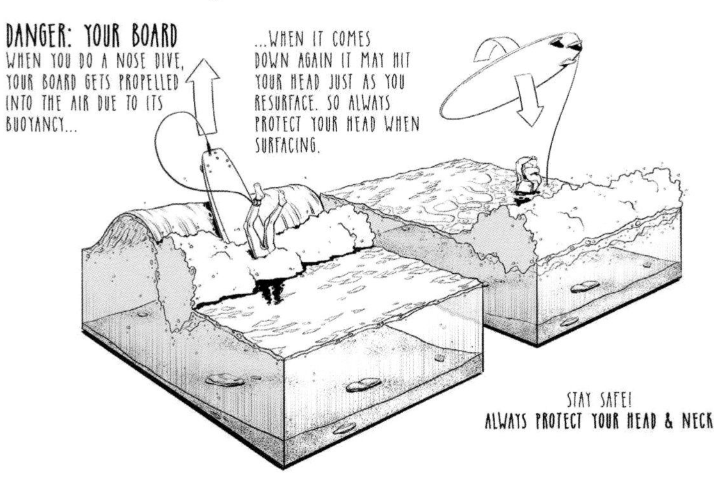

STAY SAFE!
ALWAYS PROTECT YOUR HEAD & NECK

29

HOW SURF IS CREATED

SURFABLE WAVES ARE CREATED BY STORMS OVER THE OPEN OCEAN, IDEALLY **THOUSANDS OF KILOMETERS OFF THE COAST**. THE WAVES TRAVEL FROM THERE AND ORGANIZE THEMSELVES INTO SETS OF 3–4 WAVES ALONG THE WAY. THE FURTHER THEY TRAVEL, THE CLEANER AND MORE POWERFUL THEY ARE WHEN THEY REACH THE COAST IN THE FORM OF **GROUNDSWELL**. IT IS ALSO POSSIBLE TO SURF WAVES CREATED BY STORMS CLOSER TO THE COAST, A SO-CALLED **WINDSWELL**, BUT IT WILL BE MUCH MORE MESSY AND LESS POWERFUL. HOWEVER, AS A BEGINNER ON WHITEWATER WAVES, THIS IS NOT A HUGE PROBLEM, AND YOU CAN HAVE LOTS OF FUN WITH WINDSWELL, TOO.

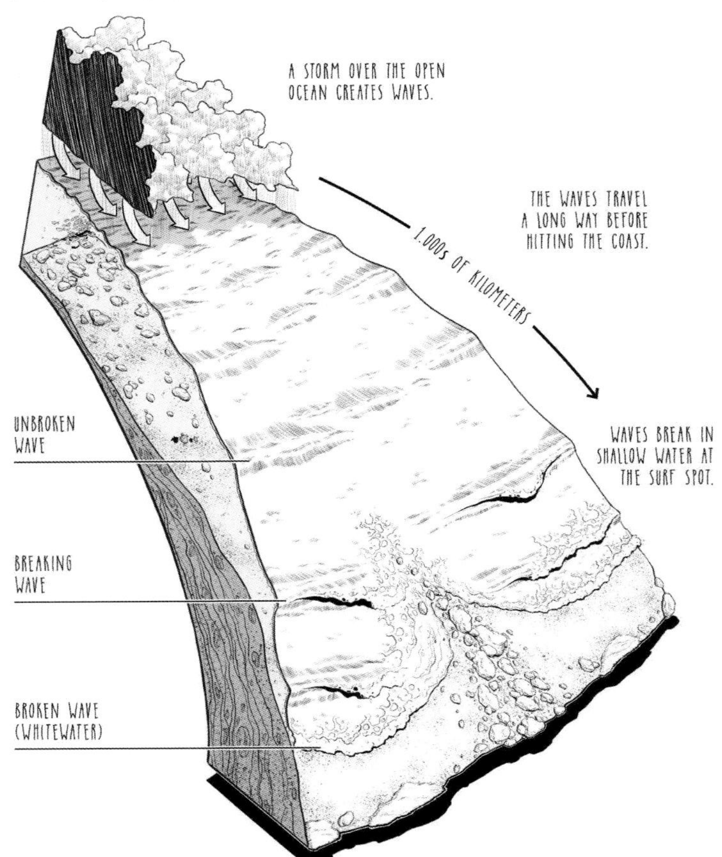

RE-ENTRY

A GOOD **BOTTOM TURN** IS THE BASIC INGREDIENT FOR ANY **TOP TURN**, E.G. THE RE-ENTRY. IT IS ALSO IMPORTANT TO PERFECTLY SYNCHRONIZE YOUR BODY **ROTATION** WITH **THROWING** YOUR ARMS TO ACCOMPLISH A POWERFUL TURN.

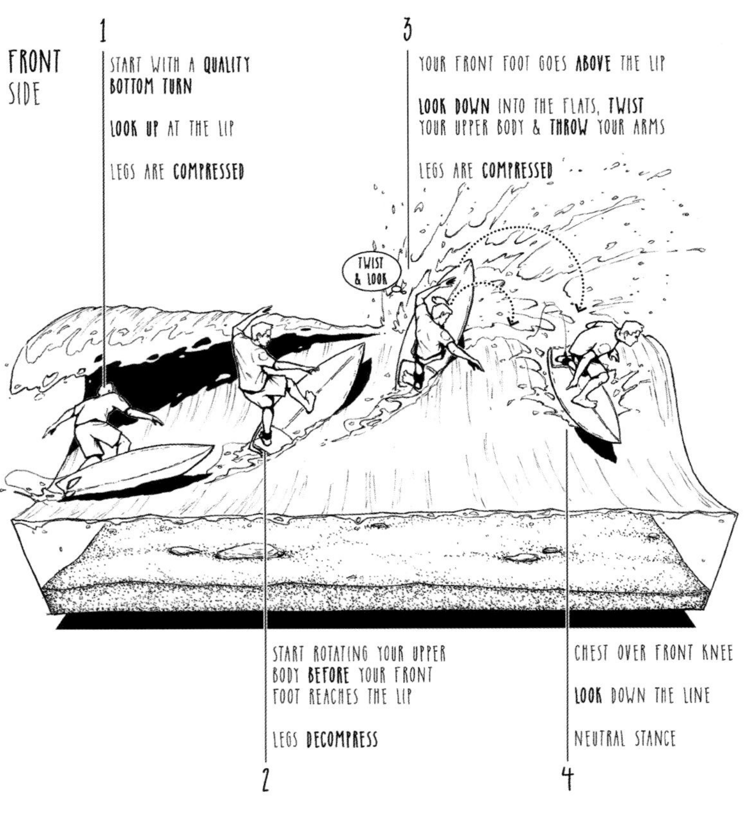

FROM PAGES TO MULTIMEDIA

THE EXPANSION OF SURF COMPANIONS

Surf Companions transcended the confines of the printed page, embracing the digital expanse to cater to the holistic needs of the modern surfer. The Companion Ecosystem burgeoned into a multifaceted platform, branching out from its literary roots into a variety of services designed to perfect the art of wave-riding. A notable milestone in this journey was the publication of "The Beginners Surf Companion", the most successful book in its genre, becoming an essential guide for surf novices, offering fundamental insights and practical advice. Daniel, leveraging his expertise as a surf photographer and videographer, propelled the brand into the visual realm with a YouTube channel. Here, he disseminated his wisdom through tutorials on surf skating, fitness, and strategic advice for navigating crowded lineups, bridging the gap between the ocean and the off-season.

The ecosystem grew, incorporating collaborations with fitness trainers and physiotherapists to produce high-quality video courses. These were meticulously crafted to optimize effectiveness, allowing surfers to train efficiently and purposefully. Beyond the screen, Surf Companions offered tangible growth through personalized coaching for surfers at all levels, integrating live video analyses available for booking through their online portal.

As the brand evolved, so did its offerings. Since 2023, Surf Companions has been organizing surf retreats, amalgamating their arsenal of coaching tools—including books like "The Beginners Surf Companion", surf skate training, professional video analysis, yoga, and physiotherapy. This holistic approach underscored their commitment to advancing a surfer's journey from foundational paddles to the mastery of towering waves, establishing Surf Companions as a beacon for surf education and lifestyle enhancement.

COMPANIONS

"Surf Companions" YouTube channel, boasting over 20,000 followers, offers a rich digital experience. It provides comprehensive tutorials, fitness tips, and strategic surfing advice, skillfully blending sea and shore wisdom. This platform is a cornerstone in their mission to enhance the surfing journey for enthusiasts worldwide.

WAVES OF THE FUTURE

CHARTING NEW WATERS IN SURF MASTERY

The horizon for Surf Companions is lined with the promise of innovation and the thrill of new frontiers in surfing education. The future teems with anticipation as the company prepares to launch the Longboard Surf Companion, a guide tailored to the elegance and style of longboard aficionados. This addition will enrich their repository of knowledge, offering nuanced expertise for those riding the gentle giants of the surfboard world.

As the tides change, Surf Companions is also set to delve into the dynamic realms of power surfing and aerial maneuvers with the upcoming Advanced Surf Companion. This volume aims to cater to the ambitious surfer, eager to conquer the competitive edge and master the psychological aspects of the sport.

Surf retreats will continue to evolve, introducing surfers to the synergistic blend of yoga and surfing, alongside the classic and soulful art of longboarding. The company is riding a wave of progression, shaping a future where every surfer, regardless of skill level, can find guidance and community within the Surf Companions ecosystem.

"Surf culture embodies a unique harmony with the sea, where each wave tells a story of adventure and freedom. It's about community, respect for nature, and the pursuit of that perfect moment where the surfer and wave become one."

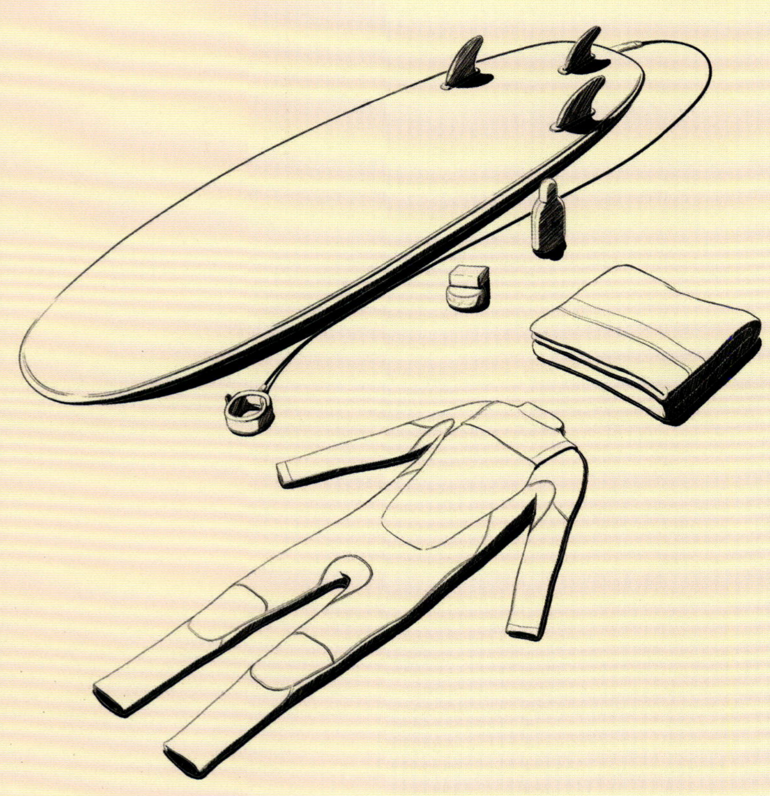

BEGINNERS
SURF
COMPANION

SURFAID

THE SURF NGO

SurfAid, a charity founded in 1999 by Dr. Dave Jenkins, is a standard bearer for the synergy between the sport of surfing and humanitarian commitment. The organization is dedicated to promoting the health, well-being and resilience of isolated communities that share a connection to surfing, concentrating its efforts primarily in the Indo-Pacific region, with a focus on Indonesia and the Solomon Islands.

The SurfAid initiative was born from the insight of Dr. Jenkins, who, after observing firsthand the precarious living conditions of isolated communities, decided to implement a distinctive intervention model. The organization focuses on providing essential services such as emergency medical care, access to clean water sources and sanitation, as well as improving the nutrition and food security of these communities.

What is remarkable about SurfAid is its strategy of community empowerment, promoting the development of lasting solutions that are culturally appropriate. A crucial part of SurfAid's work is its innovative fundraising campaigns, including the SurfAid Cup and the Make A Wave project. These campaigns manage to mobilize the global surfing community, extending the practice of sport towards an active commitment to solidarity and international cohesion.

The SurfAid story, under the leadership of Dr. Jenkins, illustrates the transformative impact that can be achieved by uniting a passion for surfing with social engagement. It represents a tale of hope and change, positively affecting both communities in vulnerable situations and the surfers who join the cause, generating a wave of positive transformations worldwide.

CATCHING WAVES, BUILDING HOPE

INTERVIEW WITH DR. DAVE JENKINS

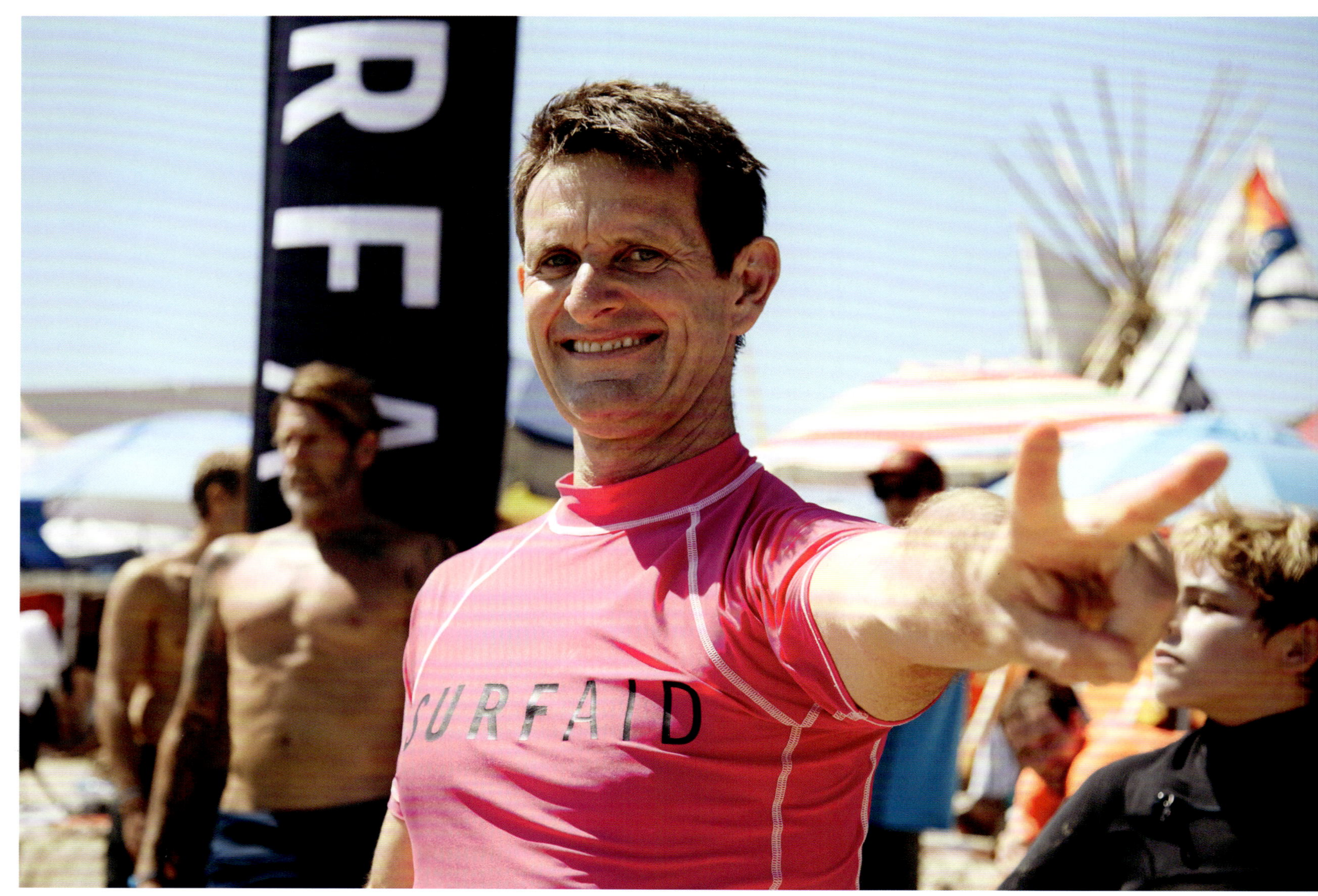

Dr. Dave Jenkins, a recognized medical expert, has devoted his career to improving health in remote communities.

What is SurfAid?

SurfAid is a global non-profit dedicated to improving the health, well-being and resilience of remote communites connected to us through surfing. Underpinning this mission is SurfAid's belief that positive, sustainable and long-lasting change can only be achieved through the active involvement of the locals in the places we love to surf.

How did the idea of SurfAid originate and what is its main objective?

It began during a 1999 surf trip I took to the Mentawais, where I was taking a break from my job as a doctor working out of Singapore. I was shocked to discover that despite being a surfing paradise, life on land was extremely tough for the locals, who were suffering from preventable and treatable diseases. The idea for SurfAid was born, with a philosophy to giving a 'hand up, not a handout' to the locals living in these remote destinations.

When did you realize it was time to change your life and help others?

The difficult scenes I witnessed in the Mentawais deeply affected me, and changed my life's direction. I left my job in Singapore, sold my house, and returned home to New Zealand. I gathered 25 friends from my local surfing crew to each pay $25 and sign up to register SurfAid as a legal non-profit.

How does surfing contribute to SurfAids cause?

At SurfAid, we like to encourage surfers to never forget the locals in the places we love to surf. In remote places like Indonesia where many surfers love to visit, there are big issues affecting the community behind the perfect waves. Supporting these communities can go a long way in providing access to healthcare, clean water, and adequate nutrition - things we often take for granted.

Was it easy to adapt to the customs and beliefs of isolated communities?

In the early days, we realised that in our impatience and fervour to help, we were missing some of the fundamentals needed to bring about real behaviour change.

We ensure that local context, local culture, and local values are at the heart and soul of our work and inform our development approach. Our local staff live and work alongside people in these communities to facilitate this slow but effective change.

What impact has SurfAid had on the prevention and treatment of diseases?

We have achieved significant outcomes in improving the capabilities of health centers, training health volunteers and midwives, establishing clean water sources, and improving food security and nutrition. Underpinning our success is the understanding that communities not only need the necessary infrastructure, but the means to become self-reliant as well.

How has SurfAid managed to reinvent itself in the face of challenges?

Over 23 years of experience in the field has taught us a lot. We make a big effort to understand the culture of the communities we work in. We listen to what the locals have to say, and to allow them to be not just a part, but the biggest part of the process. This approach has seen us continue to receive government grants and enjoy the irreplaceable support of thousands of surfers across the globe.

How do you envision SurfAid's future?

Our vision continues to be healthy and resilient communities in remote areas across the Indo Pacific Region. We will continue ensuring that children survive and thrive past the first 1,000 days of life; significantly improve the health and wellbeing of families; and ensure that community members have access to clean water and safe sanitation close to their homes.

What is the best way to support SurfAid's cause?

Our work relies on donations. Surfers can take part in our 30-day "Make a Wave" surf challenge in September or join one of our SurfAid Cup charity events in Australia and the United States. We have a monthly donation program called HandsUp, and a small donation can make a significant difference. All the information is available on our website, www.surfaid.org.

SURFAID

SURFAID

Their geographical focus on the heartlands of surfing, where few visitors but surfers venture, makes their work unique. Their program locations are in the Indo Pacific region - Indonesia (including Mentawais, Nias, Sumba, Sumbawa, and Rote) and the Solomon Islands.

SURFING FOR A CAUSE

RAISING AID THROUGH SURFING

The fundraising events organized by SurfAid constitute a fundamental aspect of their commitment to improving the quality of life in isolated communities connected to surfing. These initiatives go beyond the traditional concept of charitable events, blending sport, social cohesion, and dedication to the humanitarian cause. Annually, SurfAid hosts prominent fundraising events, with standout ones being the SurfAid Cup and the Make A Wave challenge, held in renowned surf destinations worldwide.

The SurfAid Cup, the organization's flagship event, is a team surfing tournament that brings together enthusiasts, professional surfers, and communities at large. Participating teams, united by their love for surfing, commit to raising funds, creating an atmosphere of camaraderie and competitiveness that is hard to match. This event not only aims for sporting excellence but also strives to make a real and positive impact on the lives of those in need.

On the other hand, Make A Wave is a month-long surfing challenge in September, encouraging participants to surf every day for 30 days. This challenge captures the attention of surfers of all levels, from beginners to experts, highlighting the value of perseverance towards a shared goal. This event demonstrates that daily actions can add up to achieve a significant effect.

Both initiatives exemplify SurfAid's innovative strategy in resource generation, mobilizing the enthusiasm of the global surfing community for beneficial change. The proceeds raised are directed toward funding essential projects in health, access to clean water, sanitation, and nutrition in surf-linked areas. Beyond the pursuit of the perfect wave, these events symbolize the collective effort of international surfers in supporting communities, reflecting the true spirit of solidarity and global citizenship.

SURFAID
MAKE A WAVE

SURFAID CUP

A GLOBAL FUNDRAISING SPECTACLE

The SurfAid Cup is an emblematic and fundamental fundraising event for SurfAid, an NGO committed to improving the lives of remote communities connected through surfing. Held annually at various iconic locations, including Bondi, Manly, URBNSURF in Australia, and Santa Cruz, Malibu, and Surf Ranch in the USA, this event attracts surfers of all levels, from amateurs to professionals.

In the SurfAid Cup, participating teams are made up of four friends and a professional surfer, providing a unique opportunity to surf alongside some of the sport's best. The event's tag-team style format blends camaraderie and competitive spirit to support a noble cause.

The significance of the SurfAid Cup extends beyond the sporting realm. The funds raised are crucial for SurfAid's ongoing work in providing healthcare, access to clean water and sanitation, and improving nutrition and food security in remote surfing communities. This event not only celebrates the passion for surfing but also fosters a sense of community and shared responsibility towards those less fortunate in the surf destinations many enjoy. Participating in the SurfAid Cup is a direct and joyful way to contribute to sustainable and meaningful changes in the lives of many.

SurfAid Cup Event participants as they ride the waves at Bondi Beach, a world-renowned iconic stretch of golden sands located along the picturesque coastline of Sydney, Australia.

USANA
THE CELLULAR NUTRITION COMPANY
SURFAID
CUP
ANTI VEGAN

Participants carving through the waves at URBNSURF, located just minutes from Melbourne's Tullamarine Airport.

SURFAID
FOUNDED 2000

WAVEGARDEN®
SURFAID
MAMBO

SURFAI
MAMBO

SURFAID'S MAKE A WAVE CHALLENGE

RIDING THE WAVE OF GENEROSITY

Make A Wave is SurfAid's annual peer-to-peer fundraising initiative, a unique and engaging event that embodies the spirit of the surfing community and its commitment to humanitarian efforts. Each September, participants are challenged to surf for 30 consecutive days, embracing the waves while raising funds to support SurfAid's vital programs. This initiative is open to surfers of all ages and abilities, inviting individuals, friends, families, schoolmates, colleagues, surf clubs, surf schools, and boardriding clubs to join in.

The beauty of Make A Wave lies in its simplicity and inclusivity. From young enthusiasts, known as 'super groms,' to weekend warriors, surfing moms, dads, and professional surfers, the event draws a diverse group of participants from over 28 countries. The challenge not only promotes a deeper connection with the sport but also fosters a sense of global community, united in the cause of helping others.

The funds raised through Make A Wave are instrumental in supporting SurfAid's work in remote surf communities. These contributions go towards improving healthcare, clean water and sanitation, and enhancing nutrition and food security for families living in these areas. Make A Wave is more than just a surfing challenge; it's a movement that harnesses the power of surfing to make a significant impact on the lives of those in need, illustrating how a shared passion can lead to positive global change.

“We will continue ensuring that children survive and thrive past the first 1,000 days of life; significantly improve the health and wellbeing of families; and ensure that community members have access to clean water and safe sanitation close to their homes.”

Dr. Dave Jenkins

SURFAID
CUP

IMPACT STORIES

THE HUMAN SIDE OF AID

SurfAid's impact stories demonstrate their impactful work in remote surfing communities, primarily in the Indo-Pacific region. These stories showcase how SurfAid's interventions in healthcare, nutrition, and clean water transform lives. Each case is a testament to SurfAid's commitment to empowering individuals and families, paving the way for healthier, more resilient communities.

ARLIS STORY: FOOD SECURITY AND ECONOMIC OPPORTUNITY IN THE MENTAWAI ISLANDS

Arlis, a hardworking farmer living in Bulasat Village, Mentawai Islands, along with his wife and two children, owns two hectares of land where they grow bananas, cardamom, and nuts. Their move inland after the 2010 Menatwai tsunami forced them to adapt to a new way of life, relying on farming for their livelihoods.

In 2017, Arlis learned about SurfAid through his wife's attendance at a local community health post supported by SurfAid. Subsequently, he joined a farming group facilitated by SurfAid, focused on cultivating income-generating crops like bananas. The program provided training on various farming aspects, and Arlis's dedication led to his election as the agriculture group's chair.

With 349 families participating, including Arlis and his wife, the community achieved significant progress. Today, 95% of families in the village grow bananas, and they're even planning to establish a banana flour factory, expanding economic opportunities. Thanks to SurfAid's program, the community has improved their farming methods and their overall quality of life, ensuring a brighter future for themselves and their children.

IMPROVED HEALTH OUTCOMES FOR THREE-YEAR-OLD ENI

Meet Eni, a three-year-old toddler from Bulasat Village in the Mentawai islands. She lives with her two parents and two older siblings.

Sometimes Eni has to stay with her grandmother for long periods of time while her parents travel to neighbouring hamlets and villages to maintain employment and provide for their family.

She attends the local Posyandu (or community health post) on a regular basis. Unfortunately it was observed that Eni was behind in her growth and development compared to other children her age, and was struggling to gain weight.

SurfAid worked in partnership with Eni's parents and grandmother to develop a plan to ensure she got the right mix of nutrients from a balanced diet to ensure she was gaining weight.

On returning to visit her family, Eni's growth had improved considerably. However her progress slowed when her parents were away for work, showing how meaningful the presences of her parents were to her development.

SurfAid worked with her parents through agricultural training to support them to generate a sufficient income close to home so the small family can be united on an ongoing basis and Eni and her siblings can thrive.

SURF CAMP EGYPT

MORE THAN JUST A SURF CAMP

Surf Camp Egypt represents a remarkable meeting point in the world of surfing, noted for its singular focus on integrating the rich Egyptian culture with the vibrant spirit of surfing. This camp is not only dedicated to teaching surfing, but also strives to build an inclusive and diverse community, welcoming beginners and advanced surfers alike.

What sets it apart in the global surfing landscape is its ability to offer a personalized and high quality instructional experience, adapting to the needs and abilities of each individual.

At the heart of Surf Camp Egypt is a team of experienced and passionate instructors, committed to sharing their love of surfing and promoting safe and effective learning. This commitment to excellence in instruction ensures that participants not only improve their surfing skills, but also deepen their understanding and appreciation for the sport.

The camp facilities, located at the Hacienda Red and Hacienda White properties, are strategically selected to complement the different skill levels of surfers. Hacienda Red, with its gentler waves, provides an ideal environment for beginner and intermediate surfers, while Hacienda White offers more significant challenges for more experienced surfers, with waves that test their skills and foster their development.

Beyond Egypt, Surf Camp Egypt extends its influence by organizing trips to world-renowned surf destinations such as Bali, Sri Lanka, Portugal and Morocco. These expeditions not only allow participants to explore new horizons and encounter diverse surf conditions, but also facilitate cultural exchange and a global understanding of surfing as a sport and lifestyle.

THE SURF CAMP

A PLACE TO LEARN THE SURFING LIFESTYLE

The Surf Camp offers an immersive and educational experience, positioning itself as an outstanding summer gathering for surfing enthusiasts of all levels. Located on the idyllic shores of Egypt, this camp provides a unique opportunity for participants to immerse themselves in surfing under the radiant sun and among challenging waves, creating the ideal setting for the development and passion for the sport.

The instructors, selected for their experience and teaching skills, are dedicated to providing instruction that focuses not only on technical improvement, but also on encouraging individual expression and respect for the sea and culture. This approach ensures that each participant, regardless of their initial level, can make significant progress and find their place within the world of surfing.

The Surf Camp's mission transcends mere sports practice; it strives to enrich each surfer's experience with a deeper understanding of surfing as a way of life. This involves not only learning how to maneuver in the water, but also understanding the importance of the marine environment, the history of surfing and the values of the surfing community. Interaction with instructors and other participants is designed to inspire a lasting passion for surfing, encouraging surfers to explore new frontiers and embrace the diversity of the sport.

The environment is deliberately designed to be energizing and welcoming. The intention is to create a space where positivity and camaraderie make for an unforgettable summer experience. Beginners and advanced surfers alike will find the camp an invaluable resource for perfecting their techniques, while enjoying the free and adventurous spirit that characterizes Egyptian surfing.

“The surf culture teaches us to embrace freedom, find harmony with nature, and live each day as a wave waiting to be surfed.”

OLAIAN

"It's like the mafia. Once you're in – your in. There's no getting out."

Kelly Slater

SURF SHACK

THE OASIS OF RELAXATION AND FUN AT SURF CAMP EGYPT

The Surf Shack is an emblematic creation of the Else Lab studio, conceived to offer a unique experience in the world of surfing. This space has been meticulously designed to serve as a sanctuary for wave lovers, offering a perfect balance between relaxation and human connection.

The Surf Shack is distinguished not only by its thoughtful architecture and harmonious integration with the coastal environment, but also by its commitment to the well-being and satisfaction of its visitors. Equipped with a range of first-class facilities, this retreat invites guests to enjoy a refreshing drink, to immerse themselves in the comfort of hammocks designed for absolute relaxation, or to challenge their personal balance through activities such as slackline. Each element has been carefully selected to complement the experience of disconnection and enjoyment.

Beyond being a mere space for relaxation, the Surf Shack is a meeting point for those who share an untamed passion for surfing. Here, the sun not only kisses the skin but invites relaxation and enjoyment of an environment that breathes surfing culture in every corner. The atmosphere of the place, imbued with a relaxed vibe, promotes a sense of community and belonging among visitors.

For those who seek to recharge their batteries after challenging the waves or simply want an oasis of tranquility where they can share moments with friends, the Surf Shack offers the ideal setting. This place transcends the traditional notion of a place to rest; it becomes a place of camaraderie, where laughter and stories of adventures at sea intertwine, creating lasting bonds.

CHASING THE TIDE

IN SEARCH OF THE PERFECT WAVE

Surf Camp Egypt has established itself as a leader in surf promotion, extending its programs beyond traditional seasons to offer surfers the opportunity to practice year-round. The organization has designed trips that connect participants with world-renowned surf destinations in Bali, Sri Lanka, Portugal, and Morocco, regardless of the season.

The structure of these trips includes daily surf sessions under the guidance of highly qualified instructors. Each session is planned to maximize time in the water, providing surfers of all levels the opportunity to develop their skills in various wave environments and conditions.

Additionally, the Surf Camp Egypt program offers complementary activities for a more comprehensive experience. The trips are designed not only to improve surf technique but also to provide cultural immersion. Participants can enjoy excursions to Paradise Valley, discover natural swimming spots, learn about the history and culture of cities like Marrakech, and taste local cuisine.

Surf Camp Egypt is committed to offering a complete experience that combines sport development with cultural exploration, providing surfers with a broader and enriching perspective of the world of surfing. With this approach, participants not only take away improved skills in the sport but also valuable memories and a deeper understanding of the cultures they visit.

Hurley

“When you see a wave, it may have been traveling thousands and thousands of kilometers, accumulating a unique energy. You have to know how to harness and master that energy. That's the magic of surfing.”

DLA

NATIVE

BUSTER
IX-PS FOAM

SURFING THE EISBACH

THE MUNICH RIVER WAVE

Munich reveals itself as an unexpected setting for the global surfing community, thanks to the presence of the Eisbach, a river that flows through the iconic Englischer Garten. This place stands out as a meeting point between nature and the urban environment, offering a unique and deeply rooted surfing experience in the city's character.

The Eisbach is famous for its unique artificial wave, a feature that has attracted surfers for decades. The creation of this wave is based on clever design, where strategically placed rocks on the riverbed generate a stationary wave, offering a constant and accessible challenge for surfers of varying skill levels. This phenomenon has turned the Eisbach into a living laboratory of surfing techniques, where local practitioners demonstrate remarkable mastery in conquering its dynamic current.

For those passionate about surfing, the Eisbach represents an unmissable opportunity to engage in a sport that challenges conventions, situated in the heart of one of Europe's most vibrant cities. However, the appeal of the Eisbach extends beyond the surfing community; spectators and curious onlookers regularly gather to admire the display of skill and audacity unfolding in its waters.

This cultural and sporting phenomenon in Munich underscores surfing's ability to adapt and thrive in urban environments, redefining the interactions between the city, its inhabitants, and the natural spaces that compose it. The Eisbach is not only a testament to innovation in the sport of surfing but also an emblem of the integration of urban life with a passion for outdoor activities.

“A cultural phenomenon highlighting the sport's ability to adapt to new times, new goals, and new places.”

BILLABONG

RIPCURL

Surfers take turns in a highly organized lineup, with one rider entering the wave, catching their ride, and exiting gracefully before the next surfer seizes the moment. This synchronized dance on the ever-flowing wave is a testament to the respect and camaraderie among Eisbach surfers.

The Eisbach is a magnet for surfers and tourists alike. Its unique combination of urban surroundings and a constant wave draws thrill-seekers and curious visitors to witness this captivating surf spot in the heart of the city.

With an average minimum temperature of less than 2 degrees below zero and maximum temperatures of no more than 4 degrees, winters in Munich are cold and snowfalls are common, but this does not prevent the most prepared surfers from enjoying the Eisbach.

BILLABONG

PHOTO CREDITS

BLUE WAVES SURF HOUSE
Pages 8-41: Blue Waves Surf House

ALAÏA GROUP
Pages 42-49: Alaïa Group
Page 50: Mike Wolf
Page 52: Alaïa Group
Page 54: Tomas Grootvelt
Page 56: Aurore Greindl / Mike Wolf
Page 57: Mike Wolf
Pages 58-59: Aurore Greindl
Pages 60-61: Alaïa Group
Pages 62-63: Alberto Lopes
Pages 64-65: Alaïa Group
Pages 66-67: Mike Wolf
Pages 68-69: Tomas Grootvelt

MARIONA PUJOL MERINO
Page 70: @m.w.photography.bcn
Pages 72-73: Contributor unknown
Page 74: @felipvives
Page 76: @felipvives / @gonzaloparquier
Page 77: @felipvives / @jdomenecc
Pages 78-79: @gonzaloparquier
Pages 80-81: @felipvives
Page 82: Contributor unknown
Page 83: @gerardfernandezmoll
Pages 84-85: Contributor X
Page 88: @felipvives / @paulaortegaaa

ULUWATU SURF VILLAS
Pages 90-102: Nate Lawrence
Page 103: Tommy Schultz
Page 104: Margarita Salyak
Pages 105-108: Nate Lawrence
Page 109: Angga AL
Pages 110-121: Margarita Salyak
Pages 122-125: Tommy Schultz
Page 127: Nate Lawrence
Pages 128-129: Stephen Jones

POLEN SURFBOARDS
Pages 130-143: Polen Surfboards
Pages 144-153: Hugo Almeida
Page 154: Polen Surfboards
Page 156: Vasco Lazaro
Page 158: Vasco Lazaro
Page 160: Pedro Lucas

SURF COMPANIONS
Page 162: @itsonlywater / @cokoif
Page 164: Daniel Spes
Page 165: Diriam De Vreugd
Page 166: Daniel Spes / @itsonlywater / @cokoif
Page 168: Florian Hättich
Pages 170-171: Daniel Spes
Page 172: @itsonlywater / @cokoif
Page 174: Florian Hättich
Page 175: @itsonlywater / @cokoif
Page 176: Florian's original surf notes.
Page 178: Florian's original surf notes.
Page 179: Pages from the Surf Companion books
Page 180: @itsonlywater / @cokoif
Page 182: @salty.clicks / @shannonvanegmond / Daniel Spes
Page 183: @itsonlywater / @cokoif
Page 184: @thrilledframes
Page 185: @mrjmarv
Page 186: @itsonlywater / @cokoif
Page 189: @itsonlywater / @cokoif
Page 190: Daniel Spes / @lenaluciia
Page 191: @itsonlywater / @cokoif
Page 192: Daniel Spes
Page 193: @itsonlywater / @cokoif

SURFAID
Page 194: Russell Ord
Page 203: Russell Ord
Pages 216-217: Matt Dunbar
Page 222: Russell Ord
Pages 226-229: Russell Ord

SURF CAMP EGYPT
Page 231: @gendy.yy
Pages 232-236: @maryamabdelaziiz
Page 241: @gendy.yy / @lookatmydrone
Pages 242-243: @tulipafifi
Pages 246-247: @maryamabdelaziiz

SURFING THE EISBACH
Page 260: Sigi Müller
Page 262: Luis Gervasi / F Mueller
Page 263: D. Verstl
Page 264: D. Verstl
Pages 266: Sigi Mueller / D. Verstl
Page 267: Sigi Mueller
Page 268: Werner Boehm
Page 270: Anna-Lena Zintel
Pages 272-273: Jan Saurer
Page 274: Vittorio Sciosia